pocket guide
● to ●
irish
place names

P.W. Joyce

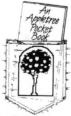

An Appletree Pocket Book

appletree press

Published and printed by
The Appletree Press Ltd
7 James Street South
Belfast BT2 8DL
1984

British Library Cataloguing in Publication Data

Joyce, P. W.
   (Irish local names explained). Pocket guide to
Irish place names.
   1. Names, Geographical—Ireland
   I. Title   II. Pocket guide to Irish place
names
   914.15′00142   DA979

   ISBN 0-86281-127-9

Contents

The author, Patrick Weston Joyce, was born in Gleno-sheen, County Limerick, in 1827. A teacher by profession, he published a number of collections of Irish songs, several histories of Ireland, and a collection of Gaelic folk-tales, as well as the popular work, *English as we Speak it in Ireland* (1910), a study of dialect variations. Perhaps his best known work, however, is *The Origin and History of Irish Names of Places* (three volumes). He died in Dublin in 1914.

This book was originally published in 1870 under the title *Irish Local Names Explained.*

Note that King's County and Queen's County are now known as Offaly and Laois respectively.

Introduction

THE PROCESS OF ANGLICISING

1. SYSTEMATIC CHANGES.

Irish pronunciation preserved: In anglicising Irish names, the leading general rule is, that the present forms are derived from the ancient Irish, as they were spoken, not as they were written. Those who first committed them to writing, aimed at preserving the original pronunciation, by representing it as nearly as they were able in English letters.

Generally speaking, this principle explains the alterations that were made in the spelling of names, in the process of reducing them from ancient to modern forms. Allowing for the difficulty of representing Irish words by English letters, it will be found that, on the whole, the ancient pronunciation is fairly preserved.

Aspiration: The most common causes of change in the reduction of Irish names, are aspiration and eclipsis. Some of the Irish consonants are, in certain situations, subject to what is called aspiration; it is indicated by the letter *h*, and it always changes the sound of the consonants.

B and *m* aspirated (*bh, mh*) are both sounded like *v* or *w*, and, consequently, where we find *bh* or *mh* in an Irish name, we generally have *v* or *w* in the English form: examples, Ardvally in Donegal and Sligo, in Irish *Ard-bhaile*, high town; Ballinwully in Roscommon, *Baile-an-mhullaigh*, the town of the summit (*mullach*). Sometimes they are represented by *f* in English, as in Boherduff, *Bothar-dubh*, black road, and often they are suppressed, especially in the end of words, or between two vowels, as in Knockdoo, *Cnoc-dubh*, black hill, the same as Knockduff in other places.

For *c* aspirated see p 7.

D and *g* aspirated (*dh, gh*), have a faint guttural sound, not existing in English, and they are consequently generally unrepresented in anglicised names, as in Lisnalee, *Lios-na-laegh*, the fort of the calves.

F aspirated (*fh*) totally loses its sound in Irish, and of course is omitted in English, as in Knockanree in Wicklow, *Cnoc-an-fhraeigh*, the hill of the heath.

P aspirated is represented by *f*, as in Ballinfoyle, *Baile-an-phoill*, the town of the hole, the same as Ballinphuill and Ballinphull elsewhere.

S and *t* aspirated (*sh, th*) both sound the same as English *h*, as in Drumhillagh in Cavan and Monaghan, *Druim-shaileach*, the ridge of the sallows, the same name as Drumsillagh in other counties, in which the original *s* sound is retained.

Eclipsis: An eclipsed consonant has its sound altogether suppressed, the sound of another consonant which is prefixed being heard instead. Thus when *d* is eclipsed by *n*, it is written *n-d*, but the *n* alone is pronounced. The eclipsed letter is of course always omitted in English.

When a noun is used in the genitive plural, with the article prefixed, its initial consonant is eclipsed. Each consonant has a special eclipsing letter of its own.

B is eclipsed by *m*. Knocknamoe, the name of a place in Queen's County, represents the Irish *Cnoc-na-mbo*, the hill of the cows.

C is eclipsed by *g*, as in Cloonnagashel near Ballinrobe, which ought to have been anglicised Coolnagashel, for the Four Masters write the name *Cuil-na-gcaiseal*, the corner of the *cashels* or stone forts.

D and *g* are both eclipsed by *n*, as in Mullananallog in Monaghan, *Mullach-na-ndealg*, the summit of the thorns or thorn bushes.

F is eclipsed by *bh*, which is represented by *v* in English, as in Carrignavar in Cork, which is in Irish *Carraig-na-bhfear*, the rock of the men.

P is eclipsed by *b*, as in Gortnaboul in Kerry and Clare, *Gort-na-bpoll*, the field of the holes.

S is eclipsed by *t*, in the genitive singular with the article, as in Ballintaggart, *Baile-an tsagairt*, the town of the priest.

T is eclipsed by *d*, as in Lisnadurk in Fermanagh *Lios-na-dtorc*, the fort of the boars.

2. CORRUPTIONS

While the majority of names have been modernized in accordance with the principle of preserving the pronunciation, great numbers on the other hand have been contracted and corrupted in a variety of ways. Some of these corruptions took place in the Irish language, but far the greatest number were introduced by the English-speaking people in transferring the words from the Irish to the English language. The following are some of the principal corruptions.

Interchange of l, m, n, r. The interchange of these letters is common in Irish and English, as well as in other languages. We find *l* very often substituted for *r*, as in

Shrule, Shruel, Struell, Sroohill, in all of which the final consonant sound should be that of *r*, for they are derived from *Sruthair* (sruher), a stream.

N is sometimes, but not often, changed to l, as in Castleconnell near Limerick, which is the castle of the O'Connings, not of the O'Connells, as the present form of the name would indicate.

The change of *n* to *r* is of frequent occurrence, as in Kilmacrenan in Donegal, which should have been called Kilmacnenan, for the Irish authorities write it *Cill-mac-nEnain*, which Colgan translates the church of the sons of Enan, who were contemporaries and relatives of St. Columba.

The change of l to *r* is not very common, but we find it in Ballysakeery in Mayo, which is written by Mac-Firbis, *Baile-easa-caoile* (Ballysakeely), the town of the narrow cataract.

M and *n* are occasionally interchanged. For example, the barony of Glenquin in Limerick, should have been called Glenquim, for the Irish is *Gleann-a'-chuim*, the glen of the *cum* or hollow. Kilmainham near Dublin is called Kilmannan by Boate, which is more correct than the present form. The name signifies the church of St. Mainen (Irish *Maighnenn*), who was bishop and abbot there in the seventh century.

Change of ch *and* th, *to* f. The guttural sound of *c* aspirated (*ch*) does not exist in English, and in anglicised names it is occasionally changed to *f*: for example, Knocktopher in Kilkenny, is from the Irish *Cnoc-a'-tochair*, the hill of the *togher* or causeway. *F* is also sometimes substituted for *th*: thus, Tiscoffin in Kilkenny took its name from an old church called *Tigh-scoithin* (Tee-Schoeen), the house of St. Scoithin, who erected his primitive church here towards the close of the sixth century.

Substitution of g *for* d. *D* aspirated is often changed to *g*, as in Drumgonnelly in Louth, which should have been anglicised Drumdonnelly, for the Irish is *Druim-Dhonghaile*, the ridge or long hill of the Donnellys.

Addition of d *after* n, *and of* b *after* m. The letter *d* is often corruptly placed after *n*—as we find in case of Rathfryland in Down, which is called in Irish *Rath-Fraeileann*, Freelan's fort. *B* is also often placed after *m*, as in Cumber or Comber, the names of several places in the northern counties. The Irish word is *Comar*, which signifies the confluence of two waters, and it is correctly anglicised Cummer and Comer in many other names.

Note

The following abbreviations have been used in quoting authorities for the Irish forms:

'F.M.,' The Annals of the Four Masters.

'Book of R.,' The Book of Rights (*Leabhar-na-gCeart*).

'Hy F.,' The Tribes and Customs of Hy Fiachrach.

'O'Dugan,' The topographical Poems of O'Dugan and O'Heeren.

'O'C. Cal.,' O'Clery's Calendar of Irish Saints, or, The Martyrology of Donegal.

'Wars of GG.,' The Wars of the *Gaedhil* with the *Gaill* (of the Irish with the Danes).

'Mart. Tam.,' The Martyrology of Tallaght.

The Irish forms are always in italics. The Irish root words are fully explained in the following section.

The pronunciation of the principal Irish words is given in brackets, as nearly as can be represented by English letters.

Irish Root Words

(The principal modern forms are given in italics)

Abh (aw or ow), a river; *aw, ow.*

Abhainn (owen), a river; *owen, avon,* and in the end of words, with the *h* of the article, *hown, hone, howna, hivnia.*

Abhall (owl, ool, or avel), an apple, an apple tree; in some parts of the north it is used in the sense of 'orchard.' Modern forms *owl, ool, owle, aval,* etc.

Achadh (aha), a field; it is generally represented in modern names by *agha, agh,* or *augh,* but these also often stand for *ath,* a ford.

Aenach (enagh), anciently signified any assembly of the people, but it is now always applied to a cattle fair; *enagh, eeny, eena, eanig.*

Aileach (ellagh), a circular stone fort; *ellagh, elly.*

Aill (oil), a cliff; *ayle, aille,* etc. *See* Faill.

Aireagal (arrigal), a habitation, an oratory, a small church; *arrigle* and *errigal.*

Airne (arney), a sloe; *arneg.*

Ait (aut), a place, a site; commonly made *at*: frequently combines with *teach,* a house, to form the compound *ait-tighe* (aut-tee), in modern forms *atty* or *atti,* a house site.

Aiteann (attan), furze; forms the terminations *-attin, -attina.*

Aith (ah), a kiln of any kind; made *-haia, -hagh, -haha, -hay, -hey,* and *-hoy,* in the end of names.

Alt, a height, a cliff, a glen side.

An, the Irish definite article.

Ar (awr), slaughter; *are, aur,* and *air.*

Ard, high, a height.

Ath (ah), a ford; *ath, ah, augh, agh, a, aha, aw,* etc.

Bád (baud), a boat.

Badhun (bawn), a cow fortress, the *bawn* of a castle.

Baile (bally), a town, a townland; *bally, balli, vally* and in the eastern counties *bal.*

Bán (bawn), white or fair coloured; *bane, baun, bawn, vane, vaun.*

Barr (baur), the top, the highest point; *bar, baur.* The *Bar* of a townland (used in the north) is the high or hilly part.

Beag (beg), little.

Bealach (ballagh), a road or pass; *ballagh, vally.*

Bealltaine (beltany), the first day of May; celebrated as a festival by the pagan Irish.

Beann (ban, ben), a horn, a gable, a peak, or pointed hill.

Beannchar (banaher), horns, gables, peaks; *banagher, bangor.*

Bearn, bearna, bearnas (barn, barna, barnas), a gap, a gap in a mountain; *barna, barny, varna, varny, barnis, varnis,* and often in the north *barnet.*

Bearnach (barnagh), gapped.

Beith (beh), the birch tree; *beitheach* (behagh) a birchy place; *behy, beha, beagh, behagh, veha, vehy,* etc.

Bél, beul (bale), the mouth, an entrance, a ford; often joined to *ath* in the compound *bél-atha* (bellaha, bella), a ford-mouth or ford entrance.

Bile (billa), a large ancient tree; a tree held in veneration for any reason; *billa, billy, villa, ville, villy, bella, vella.*

Biorar (birrer), watercress; usually corrupted to biolar (biller); *viller, vilra,* etc.

Bo, a cow; *bo, boe,* and by eclipse, *moe (mbo);* see p 6.

Boireann (burren), a large rock a rocky district.

Both (boh), a tent or hut; *bo, boh, boha, bohy, voe.*

Bóthar (boher), a road; *boher* and *voher.* In some of the eastern counties it is corrupted to *batter.* Bohereen, a little road.

Braghad (braud), the throat; a gorge: *braid, broad, braud.*

Bran, a raven.

Breach (breagh), a wolf; occurs in the compound breach- mhagh (breaghvah), wolf-field.

Bri (*bree*), a hill; *bree, bray.*

Broc (*bruck*), a badger; *brock, brick,* and, by eclipse, *mrock; see* p 6.

Brocach (bruckagh), a badger warren; *brockagh, brocky.*

Brugh (bru), a palace, a distinguished residence; *bru, bruff.* Bruighean (breean) has the same meaning; but in mod- ern times it is used to denote a fairy palace; *breen, bryan, breena, vreena.*

Buaile (boolia), a booley, a feeding or milking place for cows; *booley, boley, boola, voola, voula, vooly.*

Buidhe (bwee or boy), yellow; *boy, wee,* &c.

Buirghes (burris), a burgage or borough; *borris* and *burris.*

Bun, the end or bottom of anything; the mouth of a river.

Cabhan (cavan), a hollow; in some parts of Ulster it signi- fies a round hill; *cavan.*

Caech (kay), blind, purblind, one-eyed; *keagh, kee.*

Caenach (keenagh), moss; *keenagh.*

Caera *(kaira),* a sheep; *keeragh,* and, eclipsed with the article, *nageeragh.*

Caerthainn (kairhan), the quicken tree; *keeran, caran, kerane, keraun.*

Cairthe (carha), a pillar stone; *carra, carha,* and *car.*

Caiseal (cashel), a circular stone fort; *cashel, castle.*

Caisleán (cushlaun), a castle; *cashlaun, cashlane.*

Cala, a marshy meadow along a river or lake; a landing place for boats; *callow* and *cala.*

Capall, a horse; *capple, cappul,* and eclipsed with the article *(see* p 6), *nagappul* and *nagapple.*

Carn, a monumental heap of stones; *carn, carna.*

Carr, a rock, rocky land.

Carraig (corrig), a rock; *carrig, carrick, carriga.*

Cartron, a quarter of land (Anglo-Norman).

Casan (cassaun), a path.

Cath (cah), a battle.

Cathair (caher), a circular stone fort, a city; *caher, cahir.*

Ceallurach (calluragh), an old burial ground; *callooragh.*

Cealtrach (caltragh), an old burial ground; *caltragh caldragh.*

Ceann (can), the head, front, or highest part of anything; *kan, can, kin, ken.*

Ceapach (cappa), a plot of ground laid down in tillage; *cappagh, cappa, cap, cappy.*

Ceard (card), an artificer; *nagard, nagarde,* 'of the artificers.'

Ceardcha (cardha), a forge; *carte, cart, cartan, carton.*

Ceathramhadh (carhoo), a quarter, a quarter of land, *carrow, carhoo, carrive.*

Ceide (keady), a hillock, a hill level and smooth at top; *keady, keadew, keadagh, cady, caddagh.*

Ceis (kesh), a wicker basket, a wickerwork causeway; *kish, kesh.*

Cill (kill), a church; *kill, kil, kyle, keel, cal, kille, killa.*

Cinel (kinel), kindred, race, descendants; *kinel, kinal.*

Cladh (ely or claw), a ditch; *cly, claw, cla.*

Clann, children, a tribe; *clan, clann.*

Clar, a board, a plain; *clar, clare.*

Clais (clash), a trench; *clash.*

Cliath (clee), a hurdle.

Cloch, a stone, a stone castle; *clogh, clough, clo, clohy, cloy, naglogh.*

Clochan, a row of stepping stones across a river, sometimes a stone castle; *cloghan, cloghane, cloghaun.*

Cluain (cloon), a meadow, a fertile piece of land among bogs, marshes, or woods; *cloon, clon, clin, cloony.*

Cnap (knap), a knob, a round little hill; *knap, nap, crap, crup.*

Cnoc (knock), a hill; *knock, knick, nick, crock, cruck.*

Cobhlach (cowlagh), a fleet; *cowly, howly, coltig, holt.*

Coigeadh (coga), a fifth part, a province; *cooga, coogue.*

Coill, a wood; *kil, kyle, cuill, cullia.*

Coinieer (knickere), a rabbit warren; *coneykeare, conecar, conigar, conigare, kinnegar, nicker,* etc.

Coínín (cunneen), a rabbit; *coneen, nagoneen, nagoneeny.*

Coll, the hazel: *coll, col, cole, cull, cul, coyle, kyle, quill.*

Congbhail (congwal), a habitation, a church; *conwal, connell, cunnagavale.*

Cor, a round hill, etc.

Cora, a weir; *cor, corra, curra, cur.*

Corc, corca, race, progeny; *corka.*

Coreach, a marsh; *corcagh, corkey, cork.*

Corr, a crane or heron; *cor, gor, gore, nagor.*

Cos, a foot; *cuss, cush, cosh.*

Cot, a small boat; *cotty.*

Craebh (crave), a branch, a large brauchy tree; *creeva, crew, creevy, nagreeve.*

Craig (crag), a rock.

Crann, a tree; *crann, cran, crin, nagran.*

Crannog, an artificial island or lake dwelling; *crannoge, cronoge.*

Creabhar (crour), a wood-cock; *crour, nagrour.*

Creamh (crav), wild garlic.

Croch, a cross, a gallows, *crogh, crohy, crehy, creha.*

Crochaire (crohera), a hangman; *croghera, croghery, nagroghery.*

Cros, a cross; *cross, crush, crusha.*

Cruach, cruachán (cruagh, cruhaun), a rick, a round stacked up hill; *crogh, cruagh, croagh, croghan, croaghan*

Cruit (crit), a hump, a round little hill; *cruit, crotta, crutta, crit.*

Cu, a fierce dog, a hound: genitive *con; con, nagon, nagun.*

Cuas (coose), a cave, a cove; *coos, coose, cose, couse, goose, gose, nagoose.*

Cuil (cooil), a corner, an angle; *cool, cole.*

Cuillionn (cullion), holly; *cullion, cullen.*

Cúm (coom), a hollow, a dell or valley enclosed, except on one side, by mountains; *coom, coum, coombe.*

Currach, a marsh; *curragh, curry, curra.*

Da (daw), two; *da, daw, a.*

Daingean (dangan), a fortress: *dangan, dingin, dingle.*

Dair (dar), an oak; *dar, der, dara, darra, darraigh.*

Dairbhre (darrery), an oak forest, a place producing oaks; *darrery, dorrery, darraragh, derravara.*

Daire or doire (derry), an oak grove or wood; *derry, derri, der.*

Damh (dauv), an ox; *dav, dev, daw, duff, diff, aff, uff, iff,* and by eclipse, *nanav.*

Dearc, derc (derk), a cave; *derk, dirk, dark.*

Dearg (derg), red; *derg, derrig, darrig.*

Dearmhagh (darwah), oak-plain; *durrow, durra, derra.*

Disert, a desert, a hermitage; *disert, desert, dysart, dysert, ister, ester, isert, ishart, tristle.*

Domhnach (downagh), Sunday, a church; *donagh, donna, donny, don, dun.*

Draeighean, (dreean), blackthorn; *dreen, drain, drin.*

Droichead (drohed), a bridge; *droghed, drehid, drought drait.*

Druim (drum), the back, a ridge or long hill; *drum, drom, drim, drum.*

Dumha, (dooa), a burial mound; *dooey, dooa, doo, doe.*

Dún (doon), a fortified fort, a kingly residence; *dun, don, doon, down.*

Dur, strong.

Each (agh), a horse; *augh, agh, eigh,* etc.

Eaglais (aglish), a church; *aglish, eglish, heagles, eglir.*

Eanach (annagh), a marsh; *annagh, anna, anny.*

Eas (ass), a waterfall; *ass, ess, assy, assa.*

Eascu, eascan (asscu, asscan), an ell; *askin.*

Edar, between; *eder, ader, adder.*

Eidhneán (inaun), ivy; *eidneach* (inagh), an ivy-bearing place; *inane, inagh, eany, enagh.*

Eilit (ellit), a doe; *elty, ilty, ilt, ilt.*

Eisc (esk), a water channel; *esk.*

Eiscir (esker), a ridge of high land, a sand hill; *esker, iskera, ascragh, eskeragh.*

En (ain), a bird; *naneane,* 'of the birds.'

Eó (o), a yew tree; *o, oe, yo.*

Eochaill (oghill) a yew wood; *oghill, aughal, youghal.*

Eudan (eden), the forehead, a hill brow; *eden, edn.*

Ey (Danish), an island; *ey, i, ay, eye.*

Fada, long; *fada, fad, ad, ada, adda.*

Faeileán, faeileóg (fweelaun, fweeloge), a sea gull *naweelaun, naweeloge* ('of the sea gulls'), *wheelion, eelan.*

Faill (foyle), a cliff; *foyle, foil, fall.* See Aill.

Faithche (faha), a green level space near a residence, for games, exercises, etc.; a level field; *faha, fahy, fa, foy, fy, fey, feigh.*

Fásach (faussagh), a wilderness; *fasagh, fassagh, fassa.*

Feadán (faddaun), a streamlet; *faddan, feddan, fiddan, fiddane, eddan.*

Feadóg (faddoge), a plover; *viddoge, vaddoge, faddock, feddock.*

Feannóg (fannoge), a scaldcrow; *finnoge, funnock, vannoge.*

Fear (far), a man; fir, feara, men; *fer, fir,* and by eclipse, *navar.*

Fearann (farran), land; *farran, farn, arran.*

Fearn, fearnóg (farn, farnoge), the alder tree; *farn, fern, farnagh, ferney, farnane, farnoge, navarn, navern, navarna.*

Fearsad (farsad), a sand bank formed in a river by the opposing currents of tide and stream; *farset, farsid, farsad, fast.*

Fert, ferta, a trench, a grave; *fert, farta, ferta, fartha, arta, navart.*

Fiach (feeagh), a raven; *ee, eha, eigh, naveagh*

Fiadh (feea), a deer; *eigh, eag, nareigh.*

Fidh (fih), a wood; *fee, fi, feigh, feth, fith, fid.*

Fionn, finn (fin), white, clear, transparent; *fin, finn, fune, foun.*

Fiord (Danish), a sea inlet; *ford.*

Fórnocht, a bare, naked, or exposed hill; *forenaght, fornaght, farnaght.*

Fraech (freagh), heath; *freagh, freugh, free, ree.*

Fuaran (fooran), a cold spring; *see* Uaran.

Fuinnse, fuinnseann, fuinnseóg (funsha, funshan, funshoge), the ash tree; *funcheon, funshin, funshinagh, funchoge.* The *f* is omitted in the north, giving rise to such forms as *unshin, unshinagh, inshinagh, unshog, hinchoge.*

Gabhal (goul, gole), a fork, a river fork; *goul, gole, gowel, goole, gola.*

Gabhar (gour), a goat; *gower, gour, gore.*

Gaertha (gairha), a thicket along a river; *gearha, geragh, geeragh, gairha, geary.*

Gall (Gaul), a foreigner, a *Gaul*; a standing stone; *gall, gal, gaul, guile, gill, gullia.*

Gallán (gallaun), a standing stone; *gallon, gullane.*

Gaeth (gwee), wind; *gee, geeha, geehy, geeth.*

Gamhan (gowan), a calf; *gowan, gown.*

Gamhnach (gownagh), a milch cow, a *stripper; gownagh, gawnagh.*

Garbh (garriv), rough, rugged; *garriff, garve, garra.*

Garrán (garraun), a shrubbery; *garran, garrane, garraun, garn.*

Gárrdha (gaura), a garden; *garra, garry.*

Gédh (gay), a goose; *gay.*

Glaise, glais, gals (glasha, glash, glas), a streamlet; *glasha, glash, glas, glush.*

Glas, green; *glass.*

Gleann (glan), a glen or valley; *glen, glin, glynn, glan, glanna.*

Gniomh (gneeve), a measure of land; *gneeve.*

Gobha, gen. gobhan (gow, gown), a smith; *gow, goe, go, gown, gowan, guivna.*

Gorm, green; *gorm.*

Gort, a tilled field; *gort, gurt, gart.*

Greuch (greagh), a marshy place; *greagh, greugh.*

Graig, a village; *graigue, grag, greg.*

Grian (greean), the sun; *green, gren, greany.*

Grianan (greenan), a summer house, a palace; *greenan, greenane, greenaun, grenan, grennan.*

Guala (goola), the shoulder, a hill; *goolan, golden.*

Imleach (imlagh), a marsh on the margin of a lake or river; *emlagh, emly, imilagh.*

Inbhear (inver), the mouth of a river; *inver, enner, ineer.*

Inis (inish), an island, a low meadow along a river; *inis, inish, ennis, inch.*

Iolar (iller), an eagle; *iller, uller, ilra, ulra, illard.*

Iomaire (ummera), a ridge or long hill; *ummera, ummery, umry, amery.*

Iubhar (yure), a yew tree; *ure.*

Ladhar (lyre, lear), a fork, a fork formed by glens or rivers; *lyre, lear.*

Laegh (lay), a calf; *loe, lea, leigh.*

Lag, lug; a hollow, a hollow in a mountain; *lag, lig, leg, lug.*

Lágh (law), a hill; *law, la.*

Lann, a house, a church; *lan, lann, land, lynn, lyn.*

Lárach (lauragh), a mare; *lara, laragh.*

Lathair, lathrach (lauher, lauragh), a site, a site of a building; *laragh, lauragh.*

Lax (Danish), a salmon; *lax, leix.*

Leaba, leabaidh (labba, labby), a bed, a grave; *labba, labby.*

Leac, lic, liag (lack, lick, leeg), a flagstone; *lack, leck, lick, leek, leege.*

Leaca, Leacán (lacka, lackan), the side of a hill; *lackan, lacken, lackaun, leckan, leckaun, lacka.*

Leacht (laght), a monumental heap of stones; *laght, lat, let, lett.*

Leamh, leamhan (lav, lavaun), the elm tree; *levan, levane, livaun, laune, lamph.*

Leamhchoill (lavwhill), an elm wood; *laughil, laghil, laghile, loghill, loughill, lamfield, longfield.*

Learg, leargaidh, leargan (larg, largy, largan), the side or slope of a hill; *largy, largan.*

Leath (lah), half; *lah, la, le.*

Leathard (lahard), half height, a gentle hill; *lahard, lard.*

Léim (lame), aleap; *leam, lem, lim.*

Leithinnsi (lehinshi), half island, a peninsula; *lehinch, lahinch, lynch.*

Leitir (letter), a wet side of a hill, plural leatracha (latraha); *letter, lattera, lettera, letteragh.*

Liagán (legaun), a pillar stone; *legan, legane, legaun, leegane, leagan.*

Liath (leea), grey; *lea.*

Liathmhuine (leewinny), grey shrubbery; *leaffony, leafin, liafin, lefinn, leighmoney.*

Lios (lis), a circular earthen fort; *lis, les, lish, lass, lassa.*

Loch, a lake; *lough, low.*

Loisgreán (luskraun), corn burnt in the ear: *luskraun, loskeraun, loskeran, lustraun, lustran, lustrin.*

Loisgthe (luska), burnt, burnt land; *lusky, losky, lusk.*

Lon, londubh (lon, londuv), a blackbird; *lun.*

Long, a ship; *long.*

Longphort (longfort), a fortress; *longford, lonart, lunkard.*

Lurga, lurgan, the shin, a long low hill; *lurraga, lurgan.*

Machaire (mahera), a plain; *maghera, maghery.*

Mac-tire (macteera), a wolf; *micteera, victeera.*

Madadh, madradh (madda, maddra), a dog; *maddy, maddoo, maddra, vaddy, vaddoo, vaddra.*

Madhm (maum), an elevated mountain pass; *maum, moym.*

Mael (mwail), bald, a hornless cow, a bald or bare hill; *moyle, meel, mweel.*

Maethail (mwayhil), soft spongy land; *mohill, mothel, mothell, mehill, moyle, weehill.*

Magh (maw), a plain; *moy, ma, may, moigh, moig, muff, mo.*

Más (mauce), the thigh, a long low hill; *mace, mas, maus, mass.*

Meall (mall), a lump, a round little hill; *maul.*

Míliuc (meeluck), low marshy ground, land near a lake or river; *meelick, mellick.*

Min (meen), smooth, fine, small; *meen.*

Moin (mone), a bog; *mone, mon, mona, vone.*

Mór (more), great, large; *more, mor.*

Móta, a moat, a high mound; *moat, mota, mote.*

Mothar (moher), in the north, a cluster of trees; in the south, the ruin of a fort, or of any building; *moher.*

Muc (muck), a pig; *muck, mucky.*

Muilean (mullen), a mill; *mullen, mullin, willin.*

Muine (money), a shrubbery; *money.*

Muintir (munter), family, people; *munter.*

Muirisc (murrisk), a sea-side marsh; *murrisk.*

Mullach (mullagh), a summit; *mullagh, mulla, mully, mul.*

Murbhach (murvah), a salt marsh along the sea; *murvagh, murvey, murragh, murreagh, murrow.*

Nás (nauce), an assembly place; *naas, nash.*

Nead (nad), a bird's nest; *nad, ned, nid, neth.*

Og (oge), young, little; *oge, og, ock.*

Oileán (oilaun), an island; *illan, illane, illaun.*

Omna, an oak; *omna, umna.*

Os, a fawn; *uss, ish.*

Piast (peeast), a beast, a worm, a serpent; *piast, peastia, beast.*

Pobul (pubble), people: *pubble, pobble, popple, pobul, phubble.*

Poll, a hole; *poll, poul, pull, pool, foyle, phuill, phull.*

Preachán (prehaun), a crow; *preaghaun.*

Puca (pooka), a *pooka* or spright; *pooka, puck, pook, phuca.*

Rath (raw), a circular fort; *rath, raw, rah, ray, ra, raha.*

Reidh (ray), a coarse mountain flat; *rea, re, rey.*

Reilig (rellig), a cemetery; *relick, relig.*

Riabhach (reeagh), grey; *reagh, rea.*

Riasc (reesk), a marsh; *riesk, reisk, risk, reask.*

Rince, rinceadh (rinka), dance; *rinky, rinka, rink.*

Rinn, a point of land; *rin, rine, reen, ring, ranna.*

Ros, generally means a wood in the south, and a peninsula in the north; *ross, rus, rush.*

Rusg, a marsh; *roosk, rusk, rusky.*

Saer (sair), a carpenter; *seer, teer.*

Sagart, a priest; *saggart, taggart, teggart.*

Saileach (saulagh), a sallow; *sillagh, sallagh, sill.*

Samhuin (sowen, savin), the first of November; *souna, sawna, hawan, haman, haven, hawna.*

Scairbh (scarriff), a shallow rugged ford; *skarriff, scarry, scarva, scarvy, scarragh.*

Scairt (scart), a thicket; *scart, scarty.*

Sceach (skagh), a whitethorn bush; *skeagh, skehy, skey, ske, skeha, skew.*

Scealp (skalp), a cleft; *scalp.*

Sceilig (skellig), a rock; *skellig.*

Sceir (sker), a sharp rock, plural sceire (skerry); *sker, skerry, skerries.*

Scrin, (screen), a shrine; *skreen, skryne, skreena.*

Seabhac (shouk), a hawk; *shoke, chock, touk, tuke.*

Sealán (shallan), a hangman's rope, a gallows; *shallon, shallan.*

Sealg (shallog), hunting; *shallog, shellig.*

Sean (shan), old; *shan, shanna.*

Seiseadh (shesha), a sixth part; *shesha, sheshia, sheshiv.*

Seisreach (shesheragh), a measure of land; *sheshera, shesheragh, sistra.*

Seiscenn (sheskin), a marsh, a quagmire; *sheskin, seskin teskin.*

Sidh (shee), a fairy hill, a fairy; *shee.*

Sidheán (sheeaun), a fairy hill; *sheaun, sheehaun, sheean, shean, sion, shane.*

Siol (sheel), seed, descendants; *shil, shel.*

Sionnach (shinnagh), a fox; *shinny, shinnagh, tinny.*

Sliabh (sleeve), a mountain; *slieve, slie, sle, lieve, lie;* and by an eclipse of *s, tleva, tlieve, tlea.*

Slighe (slee), a road or pass; *slee.*

Sluagh (sloo), a host; *sloe, tloe, tloy, tlowig.*

Snamh (snauv), swimming, a swimming ford; *snauv, snave, sna, tna, tra.*

Sradbhaile (sradvally), street-town, a town with one street; *stradbally.*

Sraid (sraud), a street; *sraud, straid, strade, strad.*

Srón (srone), the nose, a nose-like hill; *sroad, shrone, stran.*

Sruth (sruh), a stream; *sruh, srue, srough, strew.*

Sruthair (sruher), a stream; shrule, shruel, struell, srool, sroohill.

Sruhán (sruhaun), a stream; *sroughan, sruffaun, straffan, truan, trone.*

Ster (Danish), a place.

Stuaic (stook), a pointed pinnacle, an out jutting point of rock; *stook.*

Suidhe (see), a sitting place, a seat; *see, se, sea, shi.*

Taebh (tave), the side, a hill-side; *teeve, teev.*

Taimhleacht (tavlaght), a plague-grave, a place where those who died of a plague were interred; *tallaght, tamlaght, tamlat, tawlaght, towlaght, toulett, howlaght, hawlagh, hamlat, hamlet.*

Tamhnach (tawnagh), a green field; *tawnagh, tawny, tonagh, tamnagh, tamny.*

Tarbh (tarriv), a bull; *tarriv, terriff, tarriff, tarf, tarry, herriff, harriff.*

Tate, tath, a measure of land; *tat, tate.*

Teach (tagh), a house; *tagh, ta, tee, ti, ty;* and by corruption, *sta, sti, sty.*

Teamhair (tawer), an elevated spot commanding an extensive view; *tara, touragh, tower, taur.*

Teampull (tampul), a church; *temple.*

Teine (tinna), fire; *tinny, tenny.*

Teotán (totaun), a burning or conflagration; *totaun.*

Tobar, tipra (gen. tioprad), a well; *tober, tubber, tipper, tubbrid, tibret.*

Tóchar (togher), a causeway over a bog or marsh; *togher.*

Tor, a tower, a tower-like rock; *tor.*

Torc (turk), a boar; *turk, torc, hirk, nadurk.*

Traigh (tra), a strand; *tra, traw, tray.*

Trian (treen), a third part; *treen, trean, trien.*

Triucha (truha), a cantred or district; *trough, true.*

Tromm, the elder or boor-tree; *trim, trom, trum.*

Tuaim (toom), a tumulus or burial mound; *toome, tom, toom, tum.*

Tuar (toor), a bleach green, any green field where things were put to bleach or dry; *toor, tore, tour.*

Tulach (tulla), a little hill; *tulla, tullow, tullagh, tully, tul.*

Turlach (toorlagh), a lake that dries up in summer; *turlough, turly.*

Ua, a grandson, a descendant; plural ui or uibh (ee, iv) descendants; *O* (in such names as O'Brien), *hy, i, ive.*

Uagh, uaimh (ooa, ooiv), a cave, gen. uamhann (ooan); forms the terminations *oe, oo, nahoe, nahoo, oova, ove, one, oon.*

Uaran (ooran), a cold spring; *oran.*

Ubhall (ool), an apple; *see* abhall.

Uisce (iska), water; *iska, isky, isk:*

Urchur (urker), a cast or throw; *urcher.*

Urnaidhe (urny), a prayer, a prayer-house or oratory, *urney,* and with the article incorporated, *nurny.*

Guide to Irish Place Names

Abbeyfeale, in Limerick: *Mainister-na-Feile*, the monastery or abbey of the river Feale.

Abbeygormican, in Galway: the abbey of the O'Cormacans.

Abbeylara (also Lara), in Longford: *Leath-rath*, F. M. (Lah-rah), half rath or fort.

Abbeyleix, the abbey of the old principality of Leix, so called from a monastery founded there in 1183 by Conor O'Moore. In the reign of Felimy the Law-giver (AD 111 to 119), this territory was given by the king of Leinster to *Lughaidh Laeighseach* (Lewy Leeshagh), Conall Carnach's grandson, for helping to expel the Munstermen who had seized on Ossory. Lewy's descendants, the O'Moores, took from him the tribe name, *Laeighis* (Leesh), and their territory was called by the same name, now modernized to Leix.

Abbeyshrule, in Longford: from a monastery founded there by one of the O'Farrells. It was anciently called *Sruthair* (Sruher), F. M., i.e. the stream, of which Shrule is a corruption.

Abbeystrowry, in Cork: the same name as the last. The *sruthair* or stream from which it was called, gave name also to Bealnashrura (the *beal* or ford-mouth of the stream) a village situated at an ancient ford.

Achonry, in Sligo: *Achadh-Chonaire* (Aha-Conary), F. M., Conary's field.

Adare, in Limerick; *Ath-dara* (Ah-dara), F. M., the ford of the oak tree. A large oak must have anciently overshadowed the old ford on the Maigue.

Addergoole (also Addragool, Adrigole, Adrigoole), *Eadar-dha-ghabhal* (Adragoul), i.e. (a place) between two (river) forks.

Aderrig, *Ath-dearg*, red ford. *See* Aghaderg.

Affane, on the Blackwater below Cappoquin: *Atha-mheadhon*, (Ah-vane), F. M., middle ford.

Agha, in several counties: *Achadh* (Aha), a field.

Aghaboe, in Queen's County, where St. Canice of Kilkenny had his principal church. Adamnan in his Life of St. Columkille, written in the seventh century, has the following passage, which settles the meaning: 'St.

Canice being in the monastery which is called in Latin *Campulus bovis* (i.e. the field of the cow), but in Irish *Ached-bou.'*

Aghaboy, *Achadh-buidhe* (Aha-boy), yellow field.

Aghacross, near Kildorrery in Cork: the ford of the cross; probably from a cross erected in connexion with St. Molaga's adjacent establishment, to mark a ford on the Funcheon. *See* Templemolaga.

Aghada, near Cork: *Ath-fhada* (Ahada), long ford.

Aghaderg, *Ath-dearg*, red ford. *See* Aderrig.

Aghadoe, near Killarney: *Achadh-dá-eó* (Aha-daw-o), F. M., the field of the two yew trees.

Aghadowey, in Derry: *Achadh-Dubhthaigh* (Ahaduffy), O'C. Cal., Duffy's field.

Achadown (also Aghadoon), the field of the *dun* or fort.

Aghadreen (also Aghadreenagh, Aghadreenan, Aghadrinagh), the field of the *dreens* or sloe bushes *(draeighean).*

Aghafad (also Aghafadda), long field.

Aghagallon, the field of the *gallan* or standing stone.

Aghagower, in Mayo: the correct name would be Aghafower, for the ancient form, as found in the old Lives of St Patrick, is *Achadh-fobhair*, the field of the spring, from a celebrated well, now called St. Patrick's well. The present form is written in Hy F., *Achadh-gabhair*, which means the field of the goat.

Aghamore, *Achadh-mór*, great field.

Aghanloo, *Athan-Lugha*, Lugh's or Lewy's little ford.

Aghavea, in Fermanagh: *Achaah-beithe* (Ahabehy), F. M., the field of the birch trees.

Achaveagh, in Donegal and Tyrone: same as last.

Aghavilla (also Aghaville, Aghavilly), *Achadh-bhile*, the field of the *bile* or old tree.

Aghaviller, in Kilkenny: *Achadh-biorair* (Ahabirrer), F. M., the field of the watercresses (*r* changed to *l*).

Aghindarragh, in Tyrone: the field of the oak.

Aghintamy, near Monaghan: *Achadh-an-tsamhaidh*, the field of the sorrel.

Aghmacart, in Queen's County: the field of Art's son.

Aghnamullen, in Monaghan: the field of the mills.

Aghnaskea (also Aghnaskeagh, Aghnaskew), *Achadh-na-sceach*, the field of the white-thorn bushes.

Aghowle, in Wicklow: *Achadh-abhla*, the field of the apple trees.

Aglish, *Eaglais* (aglish), a church.

Aglisheloghane, in Tipperary: the church of the *clogh-aun* or row of stepping stones.

Aglishcormick, in Limerick: St. Cormac's church.

Aglishdrinagh, in Cork: *Eaglais-draeighneach*, the church of the *dreens* or sloe bushes.

Agolagh, in Antrim: *Ath-gobhlach,* forked ford.

Ahane (also Ahaun), *Athán,* little ford.

Ahaphuca, the ford of the *pooka* or spright.

Ahascragh, in Galway: *Ath-eascrach,* F. M., the ford of the *esker* or sand-hill.

Aille, *Aill,* a cliff.

Allen, *Aillín,* a little cliff.

Alt, *Alt,* a height, the side of a glen.

Altan, little cliff or glen side.

Altaturk, the glen side of the boar (*torc*).

Altavilla, the glen side of the *bile* or old tree.

Altinure, *Alt-an-iubhair* (yure), the glen side of the yew tree.

Altnaveagh (also Altnaveigh), *Alt-na-bhfiach,* the cliff or glen side of the *fiachs* or ravens.

Anna, *see* Annagh.

Annabella, near Mallow: *Eanach-bile,* the marsh of the *bile* or old tree.

Annaclone, the marsh of the meadow (*cluain*).

Annacotty, near Limerick: *Ath-na-coite,* the ford of the *cot* or little boat.

Annacramph, in Armagh and Monaghan: *Eanach-creamha,* the marsh of the wild garlick.

Annaduff, *Eanach-dubh,* F. M., black marsh.

Annagh, *Eanach,* a marsh.

Annaghaskin, in Dublin, near Bray: *Eanach-easgann,* the marsh of the eels.

Annaghbeg (also Annaghmore), little marsh, great marsh.

Annahagh (also Annahaia), in Monaghan and Armagh: *Ath-na-haithe,* the ford of the kiln (*aith*).

Annahavil, *Eanach-abhaill,* the marsh of the orchard (*abhall*).

Annahilt, in Down: *Eanach-eilte,* the marsh of the doe (*eilit*).

Annakisha, the ford of the *kish* or wickerwork causeway.

Annalong, in Down: *Ath-na-long,* the ford of the ships (*long*). The ford was near the place where vessels used to be moored or anchored.

Annamoe, in Wicklow: *Ath-na-mbo,* the ford of the cows (*bo*).

Anny, *see* Annagh.

Arboe, in Tyrone: *Ard-bo,* the cow's height.

Ard, high; a height.

Ardagh, *Ard-achadh* (Ard-aha), high field.

Ardaghy, *see* Ardagh.

Ardan (also Ardane, Ardaun), little *ard* or height.

Ardara, in Donegal: *Ard-a'-raith,* the height of the rath, from a hill near the village, on which stands a conspicuous fort.

Ardataggle (also Ardateggle), *Ard-a'-tseagail,* the height of the rye (*seagal*).

Arbane (also Ardbaun), white height.

Ardbeg, little height.

Ardbraccan, in Meath: St. Brecan's height. St. Brecan erected a church here in the sixth century, some time previous to his removal to the great island of Aran, where he had his chief establishment.

Ardcarn, the height of the *carn* or monumental heap.

Ardcath, the height of the battle (*cath*).

Ardee, in Louth: Old English form Atherdee, which represents the Irish *Ath-Fhirdia* (Ahirdee), as it is written in Irish authorities, the ford of Ferdia, a chieftain who was slain there in battle by Cuchullin in the first century.

Ardeen, in Cork and Kerry: little height.

Ardeevin, *Ard-aeibhinn*, beautiful height.

Arderin, the height of Erin or Ireland.

Ardfert, in Kerry: *Ard-ferta*, F. M., the height of the grave. Sometimes called Ardfert-Brendan, from St. Brendan the navigator, who founded a monastery there in the sixth century.

Ardfinnan, in Tipperary: the height of St. Finan, who founded a monastery there in the seventh century.

Ardgeeha, *Ard-gaeithe*, height of the wind.

Ardglass, *Ard-glas*, green height.

Ardgoul, *Ard-gabhal*, high fork.

Ardkeen, *Ardcaein*, beautiful height.

Ardkill, high church or wood (*cill* or *coill*).

Ardlougher, *Ard-luachra*, rushy height.

Ardmayle, *Ard-Maille*, F. M., Malley's height.

Ardmeen, smooth height.

Ardmore, in various counties: great height.

Ardmulchan, in Meath: *Ard-Maelchon*, F. M., Maelchon's height.

Ardnacrusha (also Ardnacrushy), the height of the cross.

Ardnageeha (also Ardnageehy), the height of the wind (*gaeth*).

Ardnanean, the height of the birds (*en*).

Ardnapreaghaun, the height of the *prehauns* or crows.

Ardnarea, near Ballina: *Ard-na-riaghadh* (reea), Hy F., the hill of the executions. Four persons were executed here in the seventh century, for the murder of Kellach, bishop of Kilmore-Moy.

Ardnurcher, in Westmeath: a corruption of Athnurcher, from *Ath-an-urchair*, F. M., the ford of the cast or throw. According to a very ancient legend, a battle was fought here in the first century, between the Connaught and Ulster forces. Keth Mac Magach, a Connaught chief, threw a hard round ball at Conor mac Nessa, king of Ulster, and struck him on the head, from the effects of which the king died seven years afterwards.

Ardpatrick, St. Patrick's height.

Ardrahan, *Ard-rathain*, the height of the ferns.

Ardskeagh, the height of the *skeaghs* or bushes.

Ardstraw, in Tyrone: *Ard-sratha* (Ard-srawha), F. M., the height of (or near) the river holm.

Ardvally, in Donegal and Sligo. *See* p 5.

Ardvarna (also Ardvarness, Ardvarney, Ardvarnish), *Ard-bhearna* and *Ard-bhearnas*, high gap.

Arless, in Queen's County: *Ard-lios*, high fort.

Armagh, written in all Irish authorities *Ard-Macha*, which, in the Book of Armagh, is translated *Altitudo Machæ*, Macha's height. From Queen Macha of the golden hair, who founded the palace of Emania, 300 years BC.

Armoy, in Antrim: *Airthir-Maighe* (Arhir-moy), F. M., eastern plain.

Artimacormack, in Antrim: *Ard-tighe-Mic-Cormaic*, the height of Mac Cormack's house.

Artrea, in Derry: *Ard-Trea* (Mart. Taml.), Trea's height. The virgin St. Trea flourished in the fifth century.

Askeaton took its name from the cataract on the Deel near the town, which the F. M. call *Eas-Gephtine* (Ass-Geftine), Gephtine's cataract.

Assan (also Assaun), small *ass* or waterfall.

Assaroe, at Ballyshannon. The Book of Leinster states that *Aedh-Ruadh* (Ay-roo), queen Macha's father (*see* Armagh), was drowned in this cataract, which was thence called from him *Eas-Aedha-Ruaidh* (Assayroo), *Aedh-Ruadh's* waterfall.

Assey, on the Boyne in Meath. The F. M. record that in AD 524 'the battle of *Ath-Sithe* (Ah-Shee) was gained by *Muircheartach* (king of Ireland) against the Leinstermen, where *Sithe* (Shee) the son of *Dian* was slain, from whom *Ath-Sithe* (*Sithe's* ford) is called.'

Athenry, *Ath-na-riogh* (ree), F. M., the ford of the kings.

Athgoe, in Dublin: the ford of the *gow* or smith.

Athlacca, in Limerick: from a ford on the Morning Star river, called *Ath-leacach*, stony ford.

Athleague, in Roscommon: *Ath-liag*, F. M., the ford of the stones.

Athlone, from the ancient ford over the Shannon, called in Irish authorities *Ath-Luain*, the ford of *Luan*, a man's name.

Athneasy, in Limerick: called in the F. M., *Ath-na-nDiese* (Athnaneasy), the ford of (the tribe of) the *Desii*, who inhabited the old territory of *Deisbeag*, round Knockany.

Athnid, in Tipperary: the ford of the *nead* or bird's nest.

Athnowen, a parish near Ballincollig in Cork: from a ford on the river Bride, called *Ath-'n-uamhainn* (Ath-nooan), the ford of the cave (*uaimh*), from the great limestone cave at 'The Ovens,' near the ford.

Athy: One of the battles between Lewy and the Munstermen (*see* Abbeyleix), was fought at a ford on the Barrow, where a Munster chief, *Ae*, was slain; and from him the place was called *Ath-I* (Wars of GG), the ford of *Ae*.

Attavally, *Ait-a'-bhaile*, the site of the *bally* or town.

Atti or Atty in the beginning of a name, is the anglicised form of *áit-tighe* (aut-tee), the place or site of a house (*ait* and *teach*).

Attidermot, the site of Dermot's house.

Attiduff, the site of the black house.

Attykit, the site of *Ceat's* or Keth's house.

Aughall, in Tipperary (also Aughil, in Derry): *Eochaill*, the yew wood (*eo* and *coill*). *See* Youghal and Oghill.

Aughinish, *Each-inis*, F. M., the island of horses.

Aughnacloy, *Achadh-na-cloiche* (Ahanacloha), the field of the stone.

Aughnahoy, *Achadh-na-haithe*, the field of the kiln (*aith*).

Aughnanure, near Oughterard, in Galway: *Achadh-na-niúbhar* (Ahananure), the field of the yew trees. One of the old yews still remains.

Aughnish, *see* Aughinish.

Aughrim, the name is written in Irish document, *Each-dhruim* (Agh-rim: *dh* silent), which Colgan translates *Equi-mons*, the hill, *druim*, or ridge, of the horse (*each*).

Aughris (also Aughrus), *Each-ros*, F. M., the peninsula of the horses.

Avalbane (also Avalreagh), white orchard, grey orchard (*abhall*).

Avonmore (also Avonbeg), great river, little river (*abhainn*).

Aubeg, *Abh-bheag*, little river.

Ayle, *see* Aille.

Bahana, *see* Behanagh.

Bailey lighthouse, at Howth, from the old *bally* or fortress of Criffan, king of Ireland in the first century, on the site of which it was built.

Balbriggan, in Dublin: *Baile-Breacain*, Brecan's town.

Baldoyle, in Dublin: *Baile-Dubhghoill*, *Dubhgall's* or Doyle's town.

Balfeddock, the town of the *feadogs* or plovers.

Balgeeth, in Meath: the town of the wind (*gaeth*).

Balla, in Mayo. In the Life of St. Mochua, we are told that before the saint founded his monastery there in the seventh century, the place was called *Ros-dairbh-reach* (Ros-dar'aragh), i.e. oak grove. He enclosed the wells of his establishment with a *balla* or wall, and hence the place received the new name of Balla.

Ballagh, *Bealach,* a road or pass.

Ballaghaderreen, in Mayo: the road of the *derreen* or little oak wood.

Ballaghbehy, the road of the birch (*beith*).

Ballaghboy, yellow road (*buidhe*).

Ballaghkeen, in Wexford: beautiful road (*caein*).

Ballaghkeeran, the road of the *keerans* or quicken trees.

Ballaghmore, great road.

Ballard, *Baile-ard,* high town.

Ballee, in Down: written in the Taxation of 1306, *Baliath,* from the Irish Baile-atha, the town of the ford.

Balleen, little *bally* or town.

Ballina, the name of many places: Bel-an-atha (Bellanaha), the mouth of the ford.

Ballinabarny, the town of the *bearna* or gap.

Ballinaboy, in Cork, Galway, and Roscommon: *Bel-an-atha-buidhe,* the mouth of the yellow ford.

Ballinaclogh, the town of the stones (*cloch*).

Ballinacor (also Ballinacur, Ballinacurra), *Baile-na-corra,* the town of the weir.

Ballinafad, *Bel-an-atha-fada* (Bellanafadda), the mouth of the long ford.

Bellinagar, *Bel-atha-na-gcarr* (Bellanagar), the ford-mouth of the cars.

Ballinahinch, the town of the *inis* or island.

Ballinakill, the town of the church or wood.

Ballinalack, in Westmeath: *Bel-atha-na-leac* (Bellanalack) the mouth of the ford of the flag-stones.

Ballinalee (also Ballinalea), *Bel-atha-na-laegh,* the ford-mouth of the calves.

Ballinamona, *Baile-na-mona,* the town of the bog.

Ballinamore, *Bel-an-atha-moir,* the mouth of the great ford.

Ballinamought, near Cork: *Baile-na-mbocht,* the town of the poor people (*bocht*).

Ballinard, the town of the *ard* or height.

Ballinascarty, the town of the *scart* or thicket.

Ballinasloe, *Bel-atha-na-sluaigheadh* (Bellanaslooa), F. M., the ford-mouth of the hosts or gatherings.

Ballinaspick (also Ballinaspig), *Baile-an-easpuig,* the town of the bishop.

Ballinastraw, the town of the *srath* or river-holm.

Ballinchalla, on Lough Mask in Mayo: *Baile-an-chala,* the town of the *callow* or landing place.

Ballinclare, the town of the *clar* or plain.

Ballincloghan, *see* Ballycloghan.

Ballincollig, *Baile-an-chullaigh,* the town of the boar.

Ballincurra (also Ballincurrig, Ballincurry), *Baile-an-chur-raigh,* the town of the *curragh* or marsh.

Ballinderry, the town of the *derry* or oak wood.

Ballindrait (also Ballindrehid), *Baile-an-droichid*, the town of the bridge.

Ballineddan, in Wicklow: *Baile-an-fheadáin*, the town of the *feadan* or streamlet.

Ballinfoyle, in Galway and Wicklow; *see* p 6.

Ballingaddy, the town of the thief (*gadaighe*), i.e. the black thief O'Dwane.

Ballingarrane, the town of the *garran* or shrubbery.

Ballingarry, *Baile-an-gharrdha*, the town of the garden.

Ballinglanna (also Ballinglen), the town of the glen.

Ballingowan, the town of the smith (*gobha*).

Ballinlass (also Ballinlassa, Ballinlassy, Ballinliss), the town of the *lios* or fort.

Ballinlough, the town of the lake.

Ballinloughan (also Ballinloughaun), the town of the little lake.

Ballinlug (also Ballinluig), the town of the *lug* or hollow.

Ballinphuill (also Ballinphull), *see* p 6.

Ballinree, sometimes *Baile-an-fhraeigh*, the town of the heath (*fraech*); sometimes *Baile-an-righ*, the town of the king.

Ballinrobe, the town of the river Robe.

Ballinrostig, Roche's town.

Ballinspittle, the town of the *spital* or hospital.

Ballintaggart, *see* p 6.

Ballinteer, *Baile-an-tsaeir*, the town of the carpenter.

Ballintemple, the town of the *temple* or church.

Ballinteskin, *Baile-an-tsescenn*, the town of the morass.

Ballintlea (also Ballintleva, Ballintlevy, Ballintlieve), *Baile-an-tsleibhe*, the town of the mountain (*sliabh*).

Ballintober, the town of the well.

Ballintogher, the town of the *togher* or causeway.

Ballintubbert (also Ballintubbrid), *see* Ballintober.

Ballinure, the town of the yew tree (*iubhar*).

Ballinvally, *Baile-an-bhealaigh*, the town of the road.

Ballinvarrig (also Ballinvarry), Barry's town.

Ballinvella (also Ballinvilla), *Baile-an-bhile*, the town of the *bile* or ancient tree.

Ballinvoher, *Baile-an-bhothair*, the town of the road.

Ballinvreena, in Limerick and Tipperary: the town of the *bruighean* (breen) or fairy mansion.

Ballinwillin, *Baile-an-mhuilinn*, the town of the mill.

Ballinwully, in Roscommon: *see* p 5.

Ballytore, in Kildare, took its name from a ford on the river Greece: *Bel-atha-a'-tuair* (Bellatoor), the ford mouth of the *tuar* or bleach green.

Ballyard, high town.

Bailybaan (also Ballybane, Ballybaun), white town.

Ballybay, in Monaghan: *Bel-atha-beithe* (Bellabehy), the ford mouth of the birch.

Ballybeg, small town.

Ballyboe, i.e. 'cow-land,' a measure of land.

Ballybofey, in Donegal. The correct old name is *Srath-bofey*. Some occupier named *Fiach* or Fay must have in past times kept his cows on the holm along the Finn: *Srath-bo-Fiaich*, F. M., the river holm of Fiach's cows.

Ballyboghil, in county Dublin: the town of the *bachal* or crozier; from St. Patrick's crozier.

Ballyboley, the town of the *booley* or dairy place.

Ballybough, near Dublin: *Baile-bocht,* poor town. The same as Ballybought in other places.

Ballyboy, in King's County: written in Irish authorities *Baile-atha-buidhe* (Ballyboy) the town of the yellow ford. The name is common in other counties and sometimes means yellow town (*Baile-buidhe*).

Ballybrack, speckled town.

Ballybrannagh, Walsh's town. The proper name Walsh is in Irish *Breathnach* (Branagh), i.e. Briton.

Ballybunnion, in Kerry: Bunnion's town.

Ballycahan (also Ballycahane), O'Cahan's town.

Ballycahill, Cahill's or O'Cahill's town.

Ballycastle, in Antrim: the town of the castle.

Ballycastle, in Mayo: the town of the *cashel* or circular stone fort.

Ballyclare, *see* Ballinclare.

Ballyclerahan, in Tipperary: O'Clerahan's town.

Ballyclogh (also Ballyclohy), the town of the stones.

Ballycloghan, the town of the *cloghan* or row of stepping stones across a river.

Ballyclug, in Antrim: the town of the bell (*clog*).

Ballycolla, the town of Colla, a man's name.

Ballyconnell, in Cavan. According to tradition, Conall Carnagh, one of the most renowned of the Red Branch knights of Ulster, was slain here in the first century; hence it was called *Bel-atha-Chonaill*, the mouth of the ford of Conall.

Ballycormick, Cormac's or O'Cormac's town.

Ballycullane, O'Cullane's or O'Collins's town.

Ballydehob, in Cork: *Bel-atha-da-chab,* the ford of the two *cabs* or mouths, from some local feature.

Ballyduff, black town.

Ballyea, O'Hea's or Hayes's town.

Ballyeighter, *Baile-iochtar,* lower town.

Ballyfoyle, the town of the hole (*poll*).

Ballygarran (also Ballygarraun), the town of the *garran* or shrubbery.

Ballyglass, green town.

Ballygowan, the town of the smith (*gobha*).

Ballyheige, in Kerry: *Baile-ui-Thadg,* the town of O'Teige.

Ballyhooly, near Mallow: took its name from an ancient

ford on the blackwater, called in the Book of Lismore *Ath-ubhla* (Ahoola), the ford of the apples. The people now call it in Irish *Baile-atha-ubhla* (which they pronounce *Blaa-hoola*), the town of the apple ford, which has been shortened to the present name.

Ballykeel, *Baile-cael*, narrow town.

Ballyknock, the town of the hill.

Ballyknockan (also Ballyknockane), the town of the little hill.

Ballylanders, in Limerick: Landers's town, from an English family of that name.

Ballylig, the town of the *lug* or hollow.

Ballylongford, in Kerry: *Bel-atha-longphuirt*, the ford-mouth of the *longphort* or fortress, because it led to Carrigafoyle castle, two miles off.

Ballylough (also Ballyloughan, Ballyloughaun), the town of the lake.

Ballylusk (also Ballylusky), *Baile-loisgthe*, burnt town, from the practice of burning the surface in tillage.

Ballymena (also Ballymenagh), *Baile-meadhonach*, middle town.

Ballymoney, the town of the shrubbery (*muine*).

Ballymore, great town. Sometimes when the place is on a river it is *Bel-atha-moir* (Bellamore), the mouth of the great ford.

Ballymote, *Baile-an-mhota*, F. M., the town of the moat or mound.

Ballynabarna (also Ballynabarny, Ballynabearna), the town of the gap. *See* Ballinabarny.

Ballynaboley (also Ballynaboola, Ballynabearna), the town of the *booley* or dairy place (*buaile*). *See* Ballyboley.

Ballynacally, the town of the *calliagh* or hag.

Ballynacarrick (also Ballynacarrig, Ballynacarriga, Ballynacarrigy), the town of the rock (*carraig*).

Ballynaclogh (also Ballynacloghy), *Baile-na-cloiche*, the town of the *cloch* or stone.

Ballynacor (also Ballynacorra), the town of the weir (*cora*).

Ballynacourty, the town of the *court* or mansion.

Ballynagall (also Ballynagaul), the town of the *Galls* or foreigners.

Ballynagard, the town of the *ceards* or artificers.

Ballynagee (also Ballynageeha), town of the wind (*gaeth*).

Ballynageeragh, the town of the sheep (*caera*).

Ballynaglogh, *Baile-na-gcloch*, the town of the stones.

Ballynagore, the town of the goats (*gabhar*).

Ballynagowan, the town of the smiths (*gobha*).

Ballynagran, *Baile-na-gcrann*, the town of the trees.

Ballynahaglish, the town of the church (*eaglais*).

Ballynahinch, the town of the *inis* or island.

Ballynahone (also Ballynahown, Ballynahowna), the town of the river (*abhainn*).

Ballynahow, the town of the river (*abh*).

Ballynakill (also Ballynakilla, Ballynakilly), the town of the church or wood (*cill* or *coill*).

Ballynalacken, the town of the *leacan* or hill side.

Ballynamona, the town of the bog (*móin*).

Ballynamuck, the town of the pigs (*muc*).

Ballynamuddagh, *Baile-na-mbodach,* the town of the *bodachs* or churls.

Ballynaraha, the town of the rath or fort.

Ballynatona (also Ballynatone), the town of the *backside* or hill (*tóin*).

Ballynatray, the town of the strand (*traigh*).

Ballyneety, *Baile-an-Fhaeite,* the town of White, a family name of English origin.

Ballyness, the town of the waterfall (*eas*).

Ballynew (also Ballynoe), *Baile-nua,* new town.

Ballynure, *Baile-an-iubhair,* the town of the yew.

Ballyorgan, in Limerick: Organ's or Horgan's town.

Ballyragget, in Kilkenny: *Bel-atha-Raghat,* F. M., Ragat's ford-mouth.

Ballyroe, *Baile-ruadh,* red town.

Ballyroosky, the town of the *rusk* or marsh.

Ballysadare, in Sligo: originally *Eas-dara* (Assdara), the cataract of the oak, from the beautiful fall on the Owenmore river. It was afterwards called *Baile-easa-dara* (Ballyassadara) F. M., the town of Assdara, which has been shortened to the present name.

Ballysaggart, the town of the *sagart* or priest.

Ballysakeery, in Mayo. *See* p 7.

Ballysallagh, dirty town.

Ballyshane, Shane's or John's town.

Ballyshannon: the old ford on the Erne is called by the annalists *Ath-seanaigh* and *Bel-atha-seanaigh* (Bellashanny). From the latter, the present name is derived, and it means the mouth of *Seanach's* or *Shannagh's* ford, a man's name in common use. The *on* is a modern corruption. The peasantry call the town *Ballyshanny,* which is nearer the original. Ballyshannon in Kildare is similarly derived.

Ballytarsna (also Ballytarsney), cross-town; i.e. the village or townland had a *cross* or transverse position.

Ballyteige, O'Teige's town.

Ballytrasna, *see* Ballytarsna.

Ballyvaghan, in Clare: *Baile-ui-Bheachain,* O'Behan's town.

Ballywater, *Baile-uachtar,* upper town.

Ballywillin, the town of the mill (*muileann*).

Balrath, *Baile-ratha,* the town of the fort.

Balrathboyne, in Meath: St. *Baeithin* (Bweeheen, but often pron. Boyne), the son of *Cuana,* built a church here near an ancient rath, and the rath remains, though the church is gone. Hence it was called *Rath-Baeithin,* and in recent times, Balrathboyne, the town of *Baeithin's* rath.

Balrothery, *Baile-a'-ridire* (Ballyariddery), the town of the knight.

Baltinglass, written *Bealach-Chonglais* (Ballaconglas) in Irish authorities, the road or pass of *Cuglas,* a person about whom there is a very ancient legend.

Baltrasna, *see* Ballytarsna.

Baltray, the town of the strand (*traigh*).

Banagh, barony of, in Donegal. It is called in the annals *Baghaineach* (Bawnagh), i.e. the territory of *Boghaine* (Boana) or *Enna Boghaine,* the son of Conall Gulban, son of the great king Niall of the Nine Hostages, who reigned from AD 379 to 405.

Banagher (also Bangor), *Beannchor* (Banaher), F. M., (from the root *beann*), signifies horns, or pointed hills or rocks, and sometimes simply a pointed hill.

Bannow, in Wexford: the harbour was called *Cuan-an-bhainbh* (Coon-an-wonniv), the harbour of the *bonniv* or sucking pig, and the village has preserved the latter part of the name changed to Bannow.

Bansha, *Bainseach* (Bawnsha), a level place.

Bantry, *Beantraighe* (Bantry), Book of R., i. e. the descendants of *Beann* (Ban), one of the sons of Conor Mac Nessa, king of Ulster in the first century. A part of the tribe settled in Wexford, and another part in Cork, and the barony of Bantry in the former county, and the town of Bantry in the latter, retain their name.

Barna, *Bearna,* a gap.

Barnaboy, yellow gap.

Barnageeha (also Barnageehy), windy gap (*gaoth*).

Barnane Ely, in Tipperary: from the remarkable gap in the Devil's Bit mountain, *Bearnán-Eile,* the little gap of Ely, the ancient territory in which it was situated.

Barnes (also Barnish), *Bearnas,* a gap.

Barnismore, great gap.

Barr, the top of anything.

Baslick, *Baisleac,* F. M., a *basilica* or church.

Batterstown, the town of the *batter* (*bóthar*) or road.

Bawnmore, great green field.

Bawnoge, little green field.

Bawnreagh, greyish green field.

Baunskeha, the green field of the bush (*sceach*).

Bawnboy, yellow field.

Bawnfune, *Bán-fionn,* white field.

Bawnmore, great green field.

Beagh, *Beitheach* (Beha), a place of birches.

Bear, barony, island, and haven, in Cork. Owen More, king of Munster in the second century, spent nine years in Spain, and, according to an old legend, he married *Beara*, daughter of the king of that country. On his return to Ireland to make war against Conn of the hundred battles, he landed on the north side of Bantry bay, and called the place *Beara* in honour of his wife.

Beheenagh (also Behernagh), a place of birches (*beith*).

Behy, birch land.

Belfarsad, *see* Belfast.

Belfast. In old times the Lagan used to be crossed here by a *farset* or sandbank, and hence the place was called *Belfeirste*, F. M., the *bel* or ford of the *farset*.

Bellaghy, the mouth or entrance of the *lahagh* or slough.

Bellanacargy, in Cavan: *Bel-atha-na-cairrge*, the mouth of the ford of the rock (*carraig*).

Bellanagher, in Roscommon: *Bel-atha-na-gcarr*, the mouth of the ford of the cars.

Bellananagh, in Cavan: *Bel-atha-na-neach*, the mouth of the ford of the horses (*each*).

Bellaugh, in Roscommon: *see* Bellaghy.

Belleek, near Ballyshannon: *Bel-leice* (Bellecka), F. M., the ford-mouth of the flag stone, from the flat surfaced rock in the bed of the river. Belleek in other places is similarly derived.

Beltany, from *Bealtaine* or *Beltaine*, the first of May, because the May day sports used to be celebrated there.

Ben, a peak, a pointed hill (*beann*).

Benbo mountain near Manorhamilton, is called in Irish *Beanna-bo*, F. M., the peaks or horns of the cow, from its curious double peak.

Benburb, in Tyrone: from a cliff over the Blackwater, called in the annals *Beann-borb*, the proud peak.

Bengore head, the peak of the goats (*gabhar*).

Bengorm, blue peak.

Benmore, great peak.

Bignion (also Binnion), small *ben* or peak.

Billy, in Antrim: Bile, an ancient tree.

Binbulbin, correct name, *Binn-Gulbain*, Gulban's peak.

Bogagh (also Boggagh, Boggan, Boggaun), a boggy place.

Boher, *Bothar* (boher), a road.

Boherard, high road.

Boherboy, yellow road.

Boherduff, *see* p 5.

Bohereen, little road.

Bohermeen, smooth road.

Boherroe, red road.

Boho, in Fermanagh: *Botha* (boha), tents or huts.

Bohola, *Both-Thola,* Hy. F., *St. Tola's* hut.

Boley, *buaile,* a milking place for cattle.

Boleybeg, little *boley* or dairy place.

Boola, booley, *see* Boley.

Boolyglass, green *booley.*

Booterstown, near Dublin: the town of the *bothar, batter,* or road. In a roll of the fifteenth century it is called *Ballybothyr,* which shows that the Irish name was *Baile-an-bhothair,* the town of the road, of which the present name is a kind of half translation.

Borheen, *see* Bohereen.

Borris, *Buirghes* (burris), a *burgage* or borough.

Borris-in-Ossory, from the old territory of Ossory.

Borrisokane, O'Keane's borough town.

Borrisoleigh, from the ancient territory *Ui Luighdheach* (Hy Leea), in which it was situated.

Bourney, in Tipperary: *Boirne* (bourny), rocky lands, the plural of *Burren.*

Bovevagh, *Both-Mheidhbhe* (Boh-veva), the hut or tent of Maev or Mabel, a woman's name.

Boylagh, barony of, in Donegal: i. e. the territory of the O'Boyles.

Boyounagh, yellow *ounagh* or marsh (*abhnach*).

Braade, *see* Braid.

Brackagh(also Brackenagh, Brackernagh, Bracklagh), a speckled place, from *breac,* speckled.

Bracklin (also Brackloon), *Breac-cluain,* speckled meadow.

Braid, the, in Antrim: applied to the deep glen through which the river flows. *Braghad* (braud), a gullet or gorge.

Brandon hill in Kerry, and also in Kilkenny: both called from St Brendan the Navigator, who flourished in the sixth century.

Bray, in Wicklow: it is called Bree in old documents, and it took name from the rocky head near it: *Bri* (bree), a hill. The name of Bray head in Valentia Island in Kerry, is similarly derived.

Breaghva (also Breaghwy, Breaghy), *Breach-mhagh* (Brea-vah), the plain of the wolves (*breach,* a wolf; *magh,* a plain).

Breandrum, stinking *drum* or ridge.

Brigown, near Mitchelstown, in Cork: written *Bri-gobh-unn* (Breegown) in the Book of Lismore, the *bree* or hill of the smith (*gobha*).

Brittas, speckled land.

Britway, in Cork: *see* Breaghva.

Brockagh, a place of *brocs* or badgers.

Bruff, in Limerick: a corrupt form of *Brugh* (bru), a fort or mansion. The *brugh* is the old fort near the town.

Bruis, another form of *Brugh* (bru), a mansion.

Bruree, in Limerick: called in Irish documents *Brugh-righ* (Bruree), the fort or palace of the king, for it was the chief seat of Olioll Olum, king of Munster in the second century, and afterwards of the O'Donovans. Several of the old forts still remain.

Bullaun, *Bullán,* a well in a rock.

Bun, the bottom or end of anything; the mouth of a river.

Buncrana, the mouth of the river Crana.

Bunlahy, the end of the *lahagh* or slough.

Bunratty, in Clare: the mouth of the river Ratty, now called the Owen O'Garney.

Burren, *Boireann,* a rock, a rocky district.

Burriscara, the *burris* or borough of the old territory of Carra.

Burrishoole, derived like Burriscarra, from the territory of *Umhall* (ool) or 'The Owles.'

Burrisnafarney, in Tipperary: the *burris* or borough of the alder-plain (*see* Farney).

Buttevant, in Cork: from the French motto of the Barrys, *Boutez-en-avant,* push forward. The Irish name is Kilnamullagh, the *cell* or church of the summits (*mullach*).

Cabragh, bad land.

Caher, *cathair* (caher) a circular stone fort.

Caherbarnagh, gapped *caher* or fort: (*bearnach,* gapped).

Caherconlish, in Limerick: *Cathair-chinn-lis,* the *caher* at the head of the *lis* or fort.

Caherduggan, Duggan's *caher* or stone fort.

Cahergal, white *caher* or stone fort.

Caherkeen, in Cork: beautiful *caher* or fort.

Cahersiveen, in Kerry: it exactly preserves the pronunciation of the Irish name *Cathair-Saidhbhín,* the stone fort of *Saidhbhín,* or Sabina, a woman's name.

Cahirconree mountain, near Tralee: *Curoi's* caher, i.e. the celebrated chief, *Curoi Mac Daire,* who flourished in the first century. His caher still remains on a shoulder of the mountain.

Caldragh, *Cealdrach,* an old burying ground.

Callow, *Cala,* a marshy meadow along a river.

Callowhill, *Callchoill,* hazel wood (*coll* and *coill*).

Caltragh, *see* Caldragh.

Calluragh, *Ceallurach,* an old burial ground.

Camas (also Camus), anything that winds, a winding stream: from *cam,* crooked.

Camlin, crooked line. Often applied to a river.

Camlough, crooked lake (*cam* and *loch*).

Cappa (also Cappagh), *ceapach,* a plot of land laid down for tillage.

Cappaghbeg, little tillage-plot.

Cappaghmore (also Cappamore), great tillage-plot.

Cappaghwhite, in Tipperary: White's tillage-plot.

Capparoe, red plot.

Cappog (also Cappoge), little *cappagh* or plot.

Cappoquin, *Ceapach-Chuinn*, Conn's tillage-plot.

Caran (also Caraun), a rocky place (from *carr*).

Carbury baronies, in Longford and Sligo: so called because they were inhabited by the descendants of Carbery, one of the sons of Niall of the Nine Hostages, king of Ireland from AD 379 to 405.

Cargagh, a rock place (from *carraig*).

Cargan (also Cargin), a little rock, a rocky place.

Carha, *Cairthe* (carha), a pillar stone.

Carhoo, *ceathramhadh* (carhoo) a quarter (of land).

Carlingford, *ford* is the Danish *fiord*, a sea inlet. The old Irish name is *Cairlinn*: Carlingford, the *fiord* of *Cairlinn*.

Carlow, called in Irish documents *Cetherloch* (Caher-lough), quadruple lake (*cether*, four); the Barrow anciently formed four lakes there.

Carn, a monumental heap of stones.

Carnacally, the carn of the hag (*cailleach*).

Carnalbanagh, the carn of the *Albanach* or Scotchman.

Carnaun, little carn or monumental heap.

Carnbane, white carn (*ban* (bawn), white).

Carndonagh, in Innishowen: so called because the carn was situated in the parish of Donagh.

Carnew, *Carn-Naoi* (Nee), Naoi's carn.

Carnglass, green carn.

Carnlough, the carn of the lake.

Carnmore, great carn.

Carnsore Point. The old Irish name is *carn*, a monumental heap; the termination *ore* is Danish, and signifies the sandy point of a promontory: Carnsore is merely Carn's *ore* or sandy point of the carn.

Carnteel, in Tyrone: *Carn-tSiadhail* (Carn-teel), F. M., *Siadhal's* or Shiel's carn (*s* eclipsed).

Carn Tierna, near Fermoy. *Tighernach* (Tierna) *Tetbannach*, king of Munster in the first century, was buried under the great carn which still remains on the top of the hill; and hence the name, signifying Tierna's carn.

Carntogher hills, in Londonderry: the carn of the *togher* or causeway.

Carrantuohill, the highest mountain in Ireland. It descends on the Killarney side by a curved edge, which the spectator catches in profile, all jagged and serrated with great masses of rock projecting like teeth. *Tuathail* (thoohil) means left-handed, and is applied to anything reversed from its proper direction; *carrán* is a reaping hook; and Carrantuohill is "the reversed reaping hook," because the teeth are on a convex instead of a concave edge.

Carrick, a rock, Irish *carraig* (carrig).

The Carrick-a-Rede Rope Bridge, Co Antrim

Carrickbeg, little rock.

Carrickduff, black rock.

Carrickfergus, Fergus's rock.

Carrickmore, great rock.

Carrick-on-Shannon. Carrick is here a corruption of *carra,* a weir; and the place took its name from an ancient weir across the Shannon. Its old anglicised name was Carrickdrumrusk, properly Carra-Drumrusk, the weir of Drumrusk.

Carrick-on-Suir, the rock of the Suir; from a large rock in the bed of the river.

Carrig, a rock, *see* Carrick.

Carrigafoyle, on the Shannon, near Ballylongford: *Carraig-a'-phoill,* the rock of the hole; from a deep hole in the river, near the castle.

Carrigaholt, in Clare: written by the F. M., *Carraig-an-chobhlaigh* (Carrigahowly), the rock of the fleet; and it took its name from the rock which rises over the bay where the fleets anchored. The local pronunciation of the Irish name is Carrigaholty, from which the present name is derived. Another place of the same name which preserves the correct pronunciation, is Carrigahowly on Newport bay in Mayo, the castle of the celebrated Grace O'Malley.

Carrigaline, in Cork: the rock of O'Lehane.

Carrigallen, in Leitrim: *Carraig-áluinn,* beautiful rock; from the rock on which the original church was built.

Carrigan (also Carrigane), little rock.

Carrigans, little rocks.

Carrigdownane, Downan's or Downing's rock.

Carrigeen, little rock: **Carrigeens,** little rocks.

Carrignavar, in Cork: *see p* 6.

Carrigogunnell, near the Shannon in Limerick: *Carraig-O-gCoinneli,* F. M., the rock of the O'Connells.

Carrigroe, red rock.

Carrow, a quarter (of land). *see* Carhoo.

Carroward, high quarter-land.

Carrowbane (also Carrowbaun), white quarter-land.

Carrowbeg, little quarter-land.

Carrowcrin, the quarter-land of the tree (*crann*).

Carrowduff, black quarter-land.

Carrowgarriff (also Carrowgarve), rough quarter (*garbh,* rough).

Carrowkeel, narrow quarter (*cael,* narrow).

Carrowmanagh, middle quarter-land.

Carrowmore, great quarter-land.

Carrownaglogh, the quarter of the stones (*cloch*).

Carrownamaddoo (also Carrownamaddra, Carrowna-namaddy), the quarter of the dogs (*madadh,* and *madradh*).

Carrowntober, the quarter-land of the well (*tobar*).

Carrowreagh (also Carrowrevagh), grey quarter (*riabhach*).

Carrowroe, red quarter-land.

Cartron, an Anglo-Norman word, meaning a quarter of land.

Cashel: all the places of this name, including Cashel in Tipperary, were so called from a *caiseal* (cashel) or circular stone fort.

Cashen river, *casán* a path: for this river was, as it were, the high road into Kerry.

Cashlan, *Caislen,* a castle.

Castlebane (also Castlebaun), white castle.

Castlebar, in Mayo: shortened from Castle-Barry; for it belonged to the Barrys after the English invasion.

Castlecomer, the castle of the river-confluence (*comar*).

Castleconnell, near Limerick: *see* p 7.

Castledermot, in Kildare: The old name was Disert-dermot, Diarmad's *desert* or hermitage, from Diarmad son of the King of Ulidia, who founded a monastery there about AD 800. The present form of the name is derived from a castle built there by Walter de Riddles-ford in the time of Strongbow.

Castledillon, in Kildare: Irish name *Disert-Iolladhan* (Disertillan), *Iolladhan'* or Illan's hermitage; and the word Castle was substituted for Disert as in the last name.

Castlelyons, in Cork: the castle of O'Lehane or Lyons.

Castlemoyle, bald or dilapidated castle (*mael*).

Castlepook, the castle of the *pooka* or spright.

Castlerahan, the castle of the little rath or fort.

Castlereagh, grey castle (*riabhach*).

Castleterra, in Cavan: a corruption from the Irish *Cos-a'-tsiorraigh* (Cussatirry), the foot (*cos*) of the *searrach* or foal. The name is accounted for by a legend about a stone with the print of a colt's foot on it.

Castleventry, in Cork: the Irish name is *Caislean-na-gaeithe* (Cashlaunnageeha), the castle of the wind, of which the present name is a kind of translation.

Cavan, *Cabhan,* a hollow place. In some parts of Ulster it is understood to mean a hard round hill.

Cavanacaw, the round hill of the chaff (*cáth*); from the practice of winnowing.

Cavanaleck, the hill of the flag-stone.

Cavanreagh, grey hill (*riabhach* (reagh) grey).

Celbridge, in Kildare: the *cell, kill,* or church, of the bridge; a kind of half translation from the original Irish Irish name *Cill-droichid* (Kildrohed), the church of the *drohed* or bridge, which is still retained as the name of the parish, but shortened to Kildrought.

Cheek Point, on the Suir below Waterford: a corruption of *Sheega* Point, the Irish name being *Pointe-na-síge,* the point of the *sheegas* or fairies.

Claggan, *Claigeann,* the skull, a round hill.

Clankee, barony of, in Cavan: *Clann-an-chaoich* (*Clann-an-kee*), the *clan* or descendants of the one-eyed man. They derived this cognomen from Niall O'Reilly, slain in 1256, who was called *caech* (kee), i. e. one-eyed.

Clanmaurice, barony of, in Kerry: the *clan* or descendants of Maurice Fitzgerald.

Clanwilliam, baronies of, in Limerick and Tipperary: the *clan* or descendants of William Burke.

Clara (also Claragh), a level place; from *clar.*

Clare, a level piece of land (*clar*).

Clareen, little *clar* or level plain.

Clare-Galway. Irish name *Baile-an-chlair* (Ballinclare), F. M., the town of the plain; of which only the latter part is retained: called Clare-Galway to distinguish it from other Clares.

Clash, *Clais,* a trench or furrow.

Clashduff, black trench.

Clashganniff (Clashganniv, Clashganny), the trench of the sand, i. e. a sandpit (*gainimh* (ganniv), sand).

Clashmore, great trench.

Cleenish, *Claen-inis* (Cleeninish), sloping *inis* or island.

Cleggan, *see* Claggan.

Clifden, in Galway: a very modern corruption of the Irish name *Clochán,* which signifies a beehive-shaped stone house.

Cliffs of Moher. The term *Mothar* (Moher) is applied in the south of Ireland to the ruin of a *caher, rath,* or fort; and on a cliff near Hag's Head there stands an old stone fort, called Moher O'Ruan, O'Ruan's ruined fort, from which the cliffs of Moher received their name.

Clogh, a stone; often applied also to a stone castle.

Cloghan (also Cloghane, Cloghaun), a row of stepping stones across a river (from *cloch*).

Cloghbally, stony *bally* or townland.

Cloghboley (also Cloghboola), stony *booley* or dairy place.

Cloghbrack, speckled stone.

Cloghcor, rough stone.

Clogheen, little stone or stone castle.

Clogher, generally applied to stony land—a place full of stones; but occasionally it means a rock.

Clogherbrien, in Kerry: *Braen's* stony place.

Cloghereen, a place full of stones (*cloch*).

Cloghermore, great stony place.

Cloghernagh (also Clogherny), a stony place.

Cloghfin, *Cloch-finn,* white stone.

Cloghineely, in Donegal: *Cloch-Chinnfhaelaidh* (Clogh-Kineely), F.M., Kineely's or Mac Kineely's stone. Name accounted for by a long legend. The stone which gave name to the district is still preserved.

Cloghoge, a stony place.

Cloghpook, the *pooka's* or spright's stone.

Cloghran, *Cloichreán,* a stony place.

Cloghvoley (also Cloghvoola, Cloghvoolia, Cloghvoula), *Cloch-bhuaile,* stony *booley* or dairy place.

Cloghy, a stony place.

Clogrennan, *Cloch-grianáin,* the stone castle of the *grianan* or summer residence.

Clomantagh, in Kilkenny: Mantagh's stone castle.

Clon, a meadow. See Cloon.

Clonad, *Cluain-fhada* (Cloonada), long meadow

Clonagh, *Cluain-each,* horse meadow.

Clonallan, in Down: called by Colgan and others *Cluain-Dallain,* Dallan's meadow; from Dallan Forgall, a celebrated poet of the sixth century.

Clonalvy, *Cluain-Ailbhe, Ailbhe's* or Alvy's meadow.

Clonamery, the meadow of the *iomaire* or ridge.

Clonard, in Meath: written in Irish authorities *Cluain-Eraird,* Erard's meadow. There are several other places called Clonard and Cloonard; but in these the Irish form is probably *Cluain-ard,* high meadow.

Clonarney, *Cluain-airne,* the meadow of sloes.

Clonaslee, the meadow of the *slighe* (slee) or road.

Clonbeg, little meadow.

Clonbrock, the meadow of the *brocs* or badgers.

Cloncrew, in Limerick: *Cluain-creamha* (crawa), the meadow of wild garlic.

Cloncullen, holly meadow.

Cloncurry, shortened from *Cluain-Conaire* (Cloon-Con-ary), F. M.,Conary's meadow.

Clondalkin, near Dublin: *Cluain-Dolcain,* Dolcan's meadow.

Clonduff, in Down: *Cluain-daimh* (dav), O'C. Cal., the meadow of the ox.

Clone, a meadow: *see* Clon and Cloon.

Cloneen, little meadow.

Clonegall, in Carlow: *Cluain-na-nGall*(Cloon-nung-aul), the meadow of the *Galls* or foreigners.

Clonenagh, in Queen's County: *Cluain-eidhnech* (enagh), O'C. Cal., the meadow of ivy (*see eidhneán* in vocab.). It was so called before the sixth century, and to this day it abounds in ivy.

Clones (pronounced in two syllables), *Cluain-Eois* (Cloonoce), F. M., the meadow of *Eos* (Oce), a man's name.

Clonfad (also Clonfadda, and Cloonfad), *Cluain-fada,* long meadow.

Clonfeacle, in Tyrone: called *Cluain-fiacla* (feckla) in the Book of Leinster; the meadow of the tooth.

Clonfert: the Book of Leinster writes the name *Cluain-ferta,* the meadow of the grave.

Clongill, *Cluain-Gaill,* the meadow of the foreigner.

Clongowes, the meadow of the smith (*gobha*).

Clonkeen, *Cluain-caein* (keen), beautiful meadow.

Clonlea (also Clonleigh, and Cloonlee), *Cluain-laegh* (lee),   the meadow of the calves.

Clonliff, the meadow of herbs (*lubh,* an herb).

Clonmacnoise, written in Irish documents of the eighth century *Cluain-maccu-Nois,* which was the old pagan name: it signifies the meadow of the sons of *Nos.* This *Nos* was the son of *Fiadhach* (Feeagh), a chief of the

Large round tower and crosses, Clonmacnois

tribe of *Dealbhna* or Delvin, in whose territory Clonmacnoise was situated.

Clonmeen, *Cluain-mín* (meen), smooth meadow.

Clonmel, *Cluain-meala* (malla), the meadow of honey (*mil*).

Clonmellon, *Cluain-milain,* F. M., Milan's meadow.

Clonmelsh, *Cluain-milis,* sweet meadow (from honey).

Clonmore, great meadow.

Clonmult, the meadow of the wethers (*molt*).

Clonoghil, the meadow of the yew-wood (*eóchaill*).

Clonoulty, *Cluain-Ultaigh* (ulty), the Ulsterman's meadow.

Clonshire, *Cluain-siar,* western meadow.

Clonsillá, *Cluain-saileach,* the meadow of sallows.

Clonskeagh, *Cluain-sceach,* the meadow of the white thorns.

Clontarf, *Cluain-tarbh* (tarriv), F. M., the meadow of the bulls.

Clontibret, written by the annalists *Cluain-tiobrat,* the meadow of the spring (*tipra,* same as *tobar*).

Clonturk (also Cloonturk), the boar's meadow (*torc*).

Clonty, *see* Cloonty.

Clonygowan, *Cluain-na-ngamhan* (*Cloon-nung-own*), F. M., the meadow of the calves.

Clonyhurk, *Cluain-da-thorc* (Cloonahork), F. M., the meadow of the two boars.

Cloon (also Cloone), a meadow. *See Cluain* in vocabulary.

Cloonagh, the meadow of horses (*each*).

Cloonard, *See* Clonard.

Cloonawillin, *Cluain-a'-mhuilinn,* the meadow of the mill.

Cloonbeg, little meadow.

Clooncah, the meadow of the battle (*cath*).

Clooncoose (also Clooncose), *Cluain-cuas,* F. M., the meadow of the caves.

Clooncraff, *see* Cloncrew.

Clooncunna (Clooncunnig, Clooncunny), the meadow of the firewood (*conadh*).

Cloondara, *Cluain-da-rath,* F. M., the meadow of the two raths or forts.

Cloonee (also Clooney), meadow land.

Clooneen, little meadow.

Cloonfinlough, the meadow of the clear lake.

Cloonkeen, *Cluain-caein,* beautiful meadow.

Cloonlara, the meadow of the mare (*lárach*).

Cloonlougher, the meadow of the rushes (*luachra*).

Cloonmore, great meadow.

Cloonnagashel, in Mayo. *See p 6.*

Butler tomb, Clonmel

Cloonshannagh (also Cloonshinnagh), fox meadow (*sion-nach*).

Cloonshee, the meadow of the fairies (*sidh*).

Cloonsillagh, the meadow of sallows.

Cloonteen, little meadow.

Cloonties, *Cluainte*, meadows (English plural form).

Cloontubbrid, *see* Clontibret.

Cloontuskert, *Cluain-tuaisceirt* (tooskert), F. M., northern meadow.

Cloonty, *Cluainte*, meadows, plural of *cluain*.

Cloran (also Clorane, Clorhane), a stony place (*cloch*).

Clough, a stone or stone castle.

Cloyne, in Cork: shortened from *Cluain-uamha* (Cloon-ooa), as it is written in the Book of Leinster. The name signifies the meadow of the cave (*uaimh*); and the cave is still to be seen.

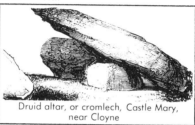

Druid altar, or cromlech, Castle Mary, near Cloyne

Clyduff, black dyke or mound (*cladh*).

Colehill, *Coll-choill,* hazel wood.

Coleraine. We are told in the Tripartite Life of St. Patrick, that a chieftain named Nadslua presented the saint with a piece of land on the bank of the river Bann, on which to build a church. It was a spot overgrown with ferns, and it happened at the moment that some boys were amusing themselves by setting them on fire. Hence the place was called *Cuil-rathain* (Coolrahen) which Colgan translates *Secessus filicis,* the corner (*cuil*) of the ferns. Coolrain, Coolrainey and Coolrah-nee, are similarly derived.

Collon, a place of hazels (*coll*).

Colp, near Drogheda. According to an ancient legend, when the Milesian brothers invaded Ireland, one of them, Colpa the swordsman, was drowned at the mouth of the Boyne; hence it was called Inver-Colpa, Colpa's river mouth; and the parish of Colp, on its southern bank, retains the latter part of the name a little short-ened.

Comber (also Comer), *see* p 7.

Commaun, a little *cum* or hollow.

Conicar (also Conicker, Conigar, Coneykeare), *Cuinicér* (cunnikere) a rabbit warren.

Conlig, the *liag* or stone of the hounds (*cu*).

Connello, baronies of, in Limerick. This was the ancient territory of the tribe of Hy Conall or *Hy Conaill Gabra* (Goura) (so written in the Book of Leinster), who were descended and named from Conall, the ninth in descent from Olioll Olum, king of Munster in the second century.

Connemara. Maev, queen of Connaught in the time of Conor mac Nessa, had three sons by Fergus mac Roy, ex-king of Ulster, namely, *Ciar* (Keer), *Con-mac*, and Modhruadh (Moroo). The descendants of *Conmac* were called *Conmacne* (*ne*, a progeny), and they were settled in Connaught, where they gave name to several territories. One of these, viz., the district lying west of Lough Corrib and Lough Mask, from its situation near the sea, was called, to distin tinguish it from the others, *Conmacne-mara* (O'Dugan: *muir*, the sea, gen. *mara*), or the sea-side *Conmacne*, which has been shortened to the present name Connemara.

Connor, in Antrim: written *Condeire* or *Condaire* in various authorities; the *derry* or oak wood of the dogs (*cu*), or as it is explained in a gloss in the Martyrology of Aengus, 'The oak wood in which were wild dogs formerly, and she wolves used to dwell therein.'

Convoy (also Conva), *Con-mhagh*, hound plain (*cu* and *magh*).

Conwal, *Congbhail* (Congwal), F. M., a habitation.

Cooga (also Coogue), *Coigeadh* (Coga), a fifth part.

Cool (also Coole), *cuil*, a corner, or *cul*, a back.

Coolattin, the corner of the furze (*aiteann*).

Coolavin, a barony in Sligo: *Cuil-O'bhFinn* (Coolovin): F. M., the corner or angle of the O'Finns.

Coolbanagher, the angle of the pinnacles. (*see* Banagher.)

Coolbane (also Coolbaun), white corner or back.

Coolcashin, Cashin's corner or angle.

Coolderry, back *derry* or oak word.

Cooleen, little corner; **Cooleeny,** little corners.

Cooleeshal (also Coolishal), low corner (*íseal*).

Cooley hills, near Carlingford. After the defeat of the Tuatha De Dananns by the Milesians, at Teltown in Meath, the Milesian chief *Cuailgne* (Cooley), following up the pursuit, was slain here; and the district was called from him, *Cuailgne*, which name is still applied to the range of hills.

Coolgreany, sunny corner or back (*grian* the sun).

Coolhill (also Coolkill), *cúl-choill*, back wood.

Coolnahinch, the corner of the *inis*, island, or river meadow.

Coolock (also Coologe), little corner or angle.

Coolroe, red corner or back.

Coom (also Coombe), *cúm*, a hollow or mountain valley.

Coomnagoppul, at Killarney: *Cum-na-gcapall*, the hollow or valley of the horses; from the practice of sending horses to graze in it.

Coomyduff, near Killarney: *Cum-ui-Dhuibh* (Coomywiv), O'Duff's valley; usually but erroneously translated Black valley.

Coos (also Coose), *cuas*, a cave.

Coosan (also Coosane, Coosaun), little cave.

Cor (also Corr). This word has several meanings, but it generally signifies a round hill.

Corballis (also Corbally), odd townland: *cor* here means odd.

Corbeagh, round hill of the birch (*beith*).

Corcomohide, in Limerick: *Corca-Muichet* (Book of Lismore), the race (*corca*) of *Muichet*, one of the disciples of the druid, *Mogh Ruith.*

Corcomroe, barony of, in Clare: *Corca-Modhruadh* or *Corcomruadh* (Corcomrua: Book of Leinster), the race (*corca*) of *Modhruadh*, son of queen Maev. (*See* Connemara.)

Corcreevy, branchy hill. *Craebh* (creeve), a branch.

Cordangan, fortified *cor* or round hill.

Cordarragh, round hill of the oak (*dair*).

Corduff, black round hill.

Corgarve, rough round hill (*garbh*).

Corglass, green round hill (*glas*).

Corick, the meeting of two rivers.

Cork, *Corcach*, a marsh. The city grew round a monastery founded in the sixth century on the edge of a marsh, by St. Finbar; and even yet a part of the city is called the Marsh.

Corkagh, *see* Cork.

Corkaguiny, barony of, in Kerry: *Corca-Duibhne* (divny: O'Dugan), the race (*corca*) of *Duibhne*, son of Carbery Musc, who was son of Conary II., king of Ireland from AD 158 to 165. *D* changed to *g*: *see* p 7.

Corkaree, barony of, in Westmeath: *Corca Raeidhe* (Ree: O'Dugan), the race (*corca*) of *Fiacha Raidhe* (Feeha Ree), grandson of Felimy the Lawgiver, king of Ireland from AD 111 to 119.

Corkeeran (also Corakeeran), the round hill of the *keerans* or quicken trees (*caerthainn*).

Corkey, *see* Cork.

Corlat, the round hill of the sepulchres (*leacht*).

Corlea, grey round hill.

Corlough, the lake of the *corrs* or herons.

Cormeen, smooth round hill.

Cornacreeve, the round hill of the branchy tree (*craebh*).

Cornagee (also Cornageeha), the round hill of the wind (*gaeth*).

Cornahoe, the round hill of the cave (*uaimh*).

Cornamucklagh, the round hill of the piggeries. *See* Mucklagh.

Cornaveagh, the round hills of the ravens (*fiach*).

Corratober, the round hill of the well (*tobar*).

Corrinshigo (also Corrinshigagh), the round hill of the ash trees. *See* Fuinnse in vocabulary.

Corrofin, in Clare: *Coradh-Finne* (Corrafinna), F. M., the weir of Finna, a woman's name.

Corskeagh, the round hill of the white thorns.

Coshbride (also Coshlea, Coshma), baronies, the first in Waterford, the others in Limerick. Cosh (Irish *cois*, from *cos* a foot), means at the foot of, near, beside. Coshbride, the barony along the river Bride. Cosh-lea, *cois-shleibhe* (cushleva), at the foot of the *sliabh* or mountain, i. e. the Galties. Coshma, *Cois-Maighe* (ma), the barony along the river Maigue.

Craan (also Craane), a stony place (from *carr*).

Crag (also Craig), other forms of *carraig*, a rock.

Cran, *Crann*, a tree.

Cranfield, a corruption of *Creamh-choill* (Cravwhill), the wood (*coill*) of wild garlic (*creamh*).

Crannagh, a place abounding in *cranns* or trees.

Crannoge, a habitation on an artificial island in a lake.

Cranny, *see* Crannagh.

Cratloe (also Crataloe), sallow wood.

Craughwell, *Creamh-choill*, wild garlic wood.

Crecora, in Limerick: *Craebh-cumhraidhe* (Crave-coory) O'Dugan, sweet scented *creeve* or branchy tree.

Creevagh, a branchy place (*craebh*).

Creeve, *Craebh* (creeve), a branch, a branchy tree.

Creevelea, grey branch or branchy tree.

Creevy, *see* Creevagh.

Creg (also Cregg), *Creag*, a rock.

Creggan (also Creggane, Creggaun), little rock, rocky ground.

Cremorne barony, in Monaghan: *Crioch-Mughdhorn* (Cree-Mourne), the country (*crioch*) of the tribe of *Mughdhorna* (Mourna), who were descended and named from *Mughdhorn* (Mourne), the son of Colla Meann, one of the three brothers who conquered Ulster, and destroyed the palace of Emania in AD 332.

Crew, *see* Creeve.

Croagh, *Cruach*, a rick or stacked up hill.

Croaghan (also Croaghaun), a round or piled up hill.

Croaghpatrick, St. Patrick's rick or hill.

Crock is very generally used in the northern half of Ireland instead of Knock, a hill.

Crockanure, *Cnoc-an-iúbhair*, the hill of the yew.

Crogh, *see* Croagh.

Croghan (also Crohane), *see* Croaghan.

Crossakeel, slender crosses.

Crossan (also Crossane, Crossaun), little cross.

Crossboyne, *Cros-Baeithin*, Hy F., *Baeithin's* or Boyne's cross.

Crosserlough, the cross on (*air*) or near the lake.

Crossgar, short cross.

Crossmaglen, in Armagh: *Cros-meg-Fhloinn* (Cros-meglin: *fh* silent), the cross of Flann's son.

Crossmolina, in Mayo: *Cros-ui-Mhaelfhina*, F. M., O'Mulleeny's or Mullany's cross.

Crossoge, little cross.

Crossreagh, grey cross (*reabhach*).

Crott, *Cruit*, a hump, a humpy backed hill.

Cruagh, *see* Croagh.

Cruit, *see* Crott.

Crumlin (also Cromlin), *Cruim-ghlinn*, (Crumlin), F. M., curved glen.

Crusheen, *Croisin*, little cross.

Cuilbeg (also Cuilmore), little wood, great wood (*coill*).

Culdaff, *Cul-dabhach* (Culdava), the back (*cul*) of the flaxdam or pool.

Culfeightrin, in Antrim: *Cuil-eachtrann* (Coolaghtran), the corner (*cuil*) of the strangers.

Cullan (also Cullane, Cullaun), a place of hazels (*coll*)

Culleen, *Coillín*, little wood.

Cullen, *Cuillionn* (Cullen), holly, holly land.

Cullenagh, a place producing holly.

Cullentra (also Cullentragh), *see* Cullenagh.

Cullenwaine, in King's County: *Cuil-O-nDubhain* (Coolonuan), F. M., the corner or angle of the O'Duanes.

Cullion, *see* Cullen.

Cully, woodland; from *coill*.

Culmullen, in Meath: the angle of the mill.

Cumber (also Cummer). *see* p 7.

Curra (also Curragh), *currach*, generally a marsh; sometimes a race course.

Currabaha (also Currabeha), the marsh of the birch.

Curraghbeg, little marsh.

Curraghboy, yellow marsh.

Curraghduff, black marsh.

Curraghlahan (also Curraghlane), broad marsh.

Curraghmore, great marsh.

Curragh of Kildare. The word here means a race course: the Curragh of Kildare has been used as a race course from the earliest ages.

Curraheen, little *currach* or marsh.

Curry, another form of Curragh, a marsh.

Cush. See Coshbride.

Cushendall, in Antrim: *Cois-abhann-Dhalla* (Cush-oundalla), the foot or termination of the river Dall.

Cushendun, in Antrim: called by the F. M., *Bun-abhann-Duine*, the end, i. e. the mouth of the river Dun; this was afterwards changed to *Cois-abhann-Duine* (Cush-oun-Dunny) by the substitution of *Cois*, the foot or end for *Bun*.

Cutteen, *Coitchionn* (cutteen), common, a commonage.

Dalkey Island near Dublin. The Irish name is *Delg-inis* (O'C. Cal.), thorn island; which the Danes, who had a fortress on it in the tenth, translated to the present name, by changing *Delg* into their word *Dalk*, a thorn; and substituting the northern word *ey*, an island, for *inis*.

Dangan, *Daingean* (dangan), a fortress.

Dangandargan, in Tipperary: Dargan's fortress.

Darragh, a place producing oaks (*dair*).

Darraragh (also Darrery), an oak forest, a place abounding in oaks (*Dairbhreach*).

Dawros, *Damhros*, the peninsula of oxen (*damh* and *ros*).

Deelis (also Deelish), *Duibh-lios* (Divlis), black *lis* or fort.

Delvin. There were formerly seven tribes called *Dealbh-na* (Dalvana), descended and named from *Lughaidh Dealbhaeth* (Lewy Dalway), who was the son of *Cas mac Tail* (seventh in descent from Olioll Olum: see Connello), the ancestor of the Dalcassians of Thomond: *Dealbhna*, i. e. *Dealbhaeth's* descendants. None of these have perpetuated their name except one, viz., *Dealbhna mor*, or the great *Dealbhna*, from whom the barony of Delvin in Westmeath received its name.

Dernish (also Derinch, Derinish), oak island (*dair*).

Derrada (also Derradd), *Doire-fhada*, long oak grove.

Derragh, *see* Darragh.

Derreen, little *derry* or oak grove or wood.

Derreens (also Derries), oak groves.

Derry, *Doire* (Derry), an oak grove or wood.

Derryad (also Derryadda), *Doire-fhada*, long oak wood.

Derrybane (also Derrybawn), whitish oak wood.

Derrybeg, little oak wood.

Derrycreevy, the oak wood of the branchy tree.

Derrydorragh (also Derrydorraghy), dark oak wood (*dorcha*)

Derryduff, black oak wood.

Derryfadda, long oak wood.

Derrygarriff (also Derrygarve), rough oak wood (*garbh*).

Derrylahan (also Derrylane), broad oak wood (*leathan*).

Derrylea, grey oak wood.

Derrylough (also Derryloughan), the oak wood of the lake.

Derrymore, great oak wood.

Derrynahinch, the oak wood of the island or river meadow (*inis*).

Derrynane, in Kerry: *Doire-Fhionain* (Derry-Eenane: *Fh* silent), the oak grove of St. Finan Cam, a native of Corkaguiny, who flourished in the sixth century.

Derrynaseer, the oak grove of the *saers* or carpenters.

Derryvullan, in Fermanagh: *Doire-Maelain* (Derry-Velan: *M* aspirated), F. M., Maelan's oak grove.

Desert, *Disert*, a desert or hermitage.

Desertcreat, corrupted from *Disert-da-Chrioch* (Disert-a-cree), F.M., the hermitage of the two territories.

Desertegny, Egnagh's hermitage.

Desertmartin, Martin's hermitage.

Desertmore, great desert or hermitage.

Desertserges, in Cork: Saerghus's hermitage.

Devenish Island, in Lough Erne: *Daimhinis* (Davinish) F. M., the island of the oxen (*damh*).

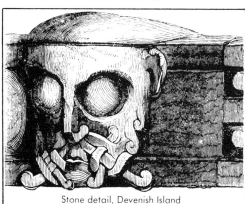
Stone detail, Devenish Island

Diamor, written in the Dinnseanchus, *Diamar*, i. e., a solitude.

Dingle, from Dingin, another form of *Daingean*, a fortress, by a change to *n* to *l* (*see* p 7). Called in the annals, *Daingean-ui-Chuis*, now usually written Dingle-I-Coush, the fortress of O'Cush, the ancient proprietor.

Dinish (also Deenish), *Duibh-inis* (Divinish), black island.

Disert, *see* Desert.

Donabate, *Domhnach-a'-bhaid*, the church of the boat.

Donagh, *Domhnach* (Downagh), a church.

Donagheloney, in Down: the church of the *cluain* or meadow.

Donaghcumper, in Kildare: the church of the *cummer* or confluence.

Donaghedy, in Tyrone: *Domhnach-Chaeide* (Donaheedy), the church of St. Caidoc, a companion of St. Columbanus.

Donaghmore, great church.

Donaghmoyne, in Monaghan: *Domhnach-Maighin*, the church of the little plain.

Donard, high *dun* or fort.

Donegal. The Danes had a settlement there before the Anglo-Norman invasion; and hence it was called *Dun-na-nGall* (Doonagall), the fortress of the *Galls* or foreigners.

Doneraile, in Cork: written in the Book of Lismore *Dun-air-aill*, the fortress on the cliff.

Donnybrook, *Domhnach-Broc*, St. Broc's church.

Donnycarney, *Cearnach's* or Carney's church.

Donohill, the fortress of the yew wood (*eóchaill*).

Donore, *Dun-uabhair* (Dunoor), F. M. the fort of pride.

Doogary, *Dubhdhoire* (Dooary), black derry or oak wood.

Doon, *Dún*, a fortress.

Doonan (also Doonane), little *dun* or fort.

Doonard, high fort.

Doonass, near Killaloe: *Dun-easa*, the fortress of the cataract, i. e. the great rapid on the Shannon.

Doonbeg, little fortress.

Doondonnell, Donall's fortress.

Dooneen, little fort.

Doonfeeny, the fort of Finna (a woman).

Doonisky (also Dunisky), the fort of the water (*uisge*).

Doonooney, Una's fort.

Douglas, *Dubh-ghlaise*, black stream.

Down, a form of *Dun*, a fortress.

Downings, *Dooneens* or little forts.

Downpatrick takes its name from the large entrenched *dun* near the cathedral. In the first century this fortress was the residence of a warrior of the Red Branch Knights, called *Celtchair*, or Keltar of the battles, from whom it is called in Irish authorities, Dunkeltar. By ecclesiastical writers it is commonly called *Dun-da-leth-glas*, the fortress of the two broken locks (*glas*) or fetters. This long name was afterwards shortened to *Dun* or *Down*, which was extended to the county. The name of St. Patrick was added, to commemorate his connexion with the place.

Downs, *duns* or forts.

Dreen, *Draeighean* (dreean), the blackthorn.

Dreenagh, a place producing blackthorns.

Dreenan, blackthorn, a place of blackthorns.

Drehidtarsna, in Limerick: cross bridge.

Dressoge (also Dressogagh), a briery or bushy place.

Dresternagh (also Dresternan, Dristernan), *see* Dressoge.

Drim, a form of *druim*, a ridge.

Drimeen (also Drimmeen), little ridge.

Drimna (also Drimnagh), ridges, a place full of ridges or hills.

Drinagh (also Drinaghan), a place producing *dreens* or blackthorns.

Drinan (also Drinaun), *see* Dreenan.

Drishaghaun (also Drishane, Drishoge), *see* Dressoge.

Droghed, *Droichead,* a bridge.

Drogheda, *Droiched-atha* (Drohedaha), F. M., the bridge of the ford; from the ford across the Boyne, used before the erection of a bridge.

Drom, *Druim,* a ridge or long hill.

Dromada (also Dromadda), long *drum* or ridge.

Drombeg (also Drumbeg), small ridge.

Dromcolliher, in Limerick: a corruption of *Druim-Coll-choille* (Drum-Collohill), the ridge of the hazel wood.

Dromdaleague, in Cork: the ridge of the two *liags* or pillar stones.

Dromgarriff, rough ridge.

Dromin, *see* Drom.

Dromineer, in Tipperary: *Druim-inbhir* (Druminver), the ridge of the *inver* or river mouth: because it is situated near where the Nenagh river enters Lough Derg.

Dromkeen, beautiful ridge.

Dromore, great ridge or long hill.

Dromtrasna, cross ridge.

Drum, *Druim,* a ridge or long hill.

Drumad, *Druim-fhada,* long ridge.

Dromadoon, the ridge of the *dun* or fort.

Drumahaire, in Leitrim: *Druim-da-ethiar* (Drum-a-ehir), F. M., the ridge of the two air-demons.

Drumanure, the ridge of the yew tree.

Drumany (also Drummany), ridges, ridged land.

Drumard, high ridge or long hill.

Drumatemple, the ridge of the temple or church.

Drumavaddy, the ridge of the dog (*madadh*).

Drumballyroney, the ridge of O'Roney's town.

Drumbane (also Drumbaun), white ridge.

Drumbarnet, the ridge of the gap (*bearna*).

Drumbo (also Drumboe), *Druimbo,* F. M., the cow's ridge.

Drumbrughas, the ridge of the farm-house.

Drumcanon, the ridge of the white-faced cow: *ceann-fhionn* (canon), whitehead

Drumcar, in Louth: *Druim-caradh* (Drumcara) F. M., the ridge of the weir.

Drumcliff, in Sligo: *Drium-chliabh* (Drumcleev), F. M., the ridge of the baskets.

Drumcolumb, St. Columba's ridge.

Drumcondra, Conra's ridge.

Drumcrin, the ridge of the tree (*crann*).

Drumcrow, the ridge of the cattle sheds (*cro*).

Drumcullen (also Drumcullion), the ridge of holly.

Drumderg, *Druim-dearg,* red ridge.

Drumduff, *Druim-dubh,* black ridge.

Drumfad, *Druim-fada,* long ridge.

Drumgill, the ridge of the *Gall* or foreigner.

Drumgoose (also Drumgose), the ridge of the caves (*cuas*).

Drumgowna (also Drumgownagh), *Druim-gamhnach,* the ridge of the heifers.

Drumharrif (Drumherriff), *Druim-thairbh* (Drum-har-riv), the ridge of the bull.

Drumhillagh, *see* p 6.

Drumhirk, *Druim-thuirc,* the ridge of the boar.

Drumhome, in Donegal. In O'C. Cal. the name is written *Druim-Thuama* (Drumhooma), and Adam-nan translates it *Dorsum Tommae,* the ridge of Tomma, a pagan woman's name.

Drumillard (also Drummillar), the eagle's ridge (*iolar*).

Drumkeen, beautiful ridge.

Drumkeeran, the ridge of the quicken trees.

Drumlane, *Druim-leathan* (lahan), F. M., broad ridge.

Drumlease, *Druim-lias,* the ridge of the huts.

Drumlish, the ridge of the *lis* or fort.

Drumlougher, the ridge of the rushes (*luachra*).

Drumman, *see* Drum.

Drummeen, little ridge.

Drummin, *see* Drum.

Drummond, a corrupt form of Drumman. *See* p 7.

Drummuck, the ridge of the pigs (*muc*).

Drummully, the ridge of the summit (*mullach*).

Drumnacross, the ridge of the cross.

Drumneen, little ridge.

Drumquin, *Druim-Chuinn,* Conn's ridge.

Drumraine (also Drumrainy), ferny ridge (*ráthain*).

Drumreagh, *Druim-riabbach,* grey ridge.

Drumroe, *Druim-ruadh,* red ridge.

Drumroosk, the ridge of the *roosk* or marsh.

Drumshallon, the ridge of the gallows (*sealan*).

Drumshanbo, the ridge of the old *both* or tent (*sean,* old).

Drumsillagh, *see* p 6.

Drumsna (also Drumsnauv), *Druim-snamha* (snawa), the ridge of the swimming. *See* Lixnaw.

Drumsurn, the ridge of the furnace or kiln (*sorn*).

Duagh, in Kerry: *Dubh-ath* (Dooah), black ford, from a ford on the river Feale.

Dublin. The name is written in the annals *Duibh-linn* (Duvlin), which, in some of the Latin Lives of the saints, is translated *Nigra therma,* black pool; it was originally the name of that part of the Liffey on which the city is built, and is sufficiently descriptive at the present day. In very early ages an artificial ford of hurdles was constructed across the Liffey, where the main road from

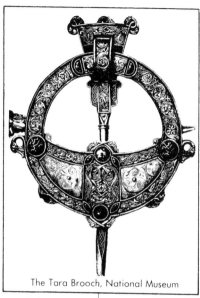

The Tara Brooch, National Museum

Tara to Wicklow crossed the river; and the city that subsequently sprung up around it was called from this circumstance *Ath-cliath* (Ah-clee), F. M., the ford of hurdles, which was the ancient name of Dublin. This name is still used by speakers of Irish in every part of Ireland; but they join it to Bally—*Baile-atha-cliath* (which they pronounce *Blaa-clee*), the town of the hurdle ford.

Dufferin, barony of, in Down: *Dubh-thrian* (Duv-reen), F. M., the black *treen* or third part.

Duhallow, in Cork: *Duthaigh-Ealla* (Doohy-alla), F. M., the district of the Allo, from the Blackwater river, a portion of which was anciently called the Allo.

Dulane, in Meath: *Tuilen,* F. M., little *tulach* or hill.

Duleek, in Meath: *Daimhliag* (Davleeg), O'C. Cal., stone house or church (*daimh*, a house, and *liag*).

Dunamase, in Queen's County: should have been called Dunmask, for the Irish name is *Dun-Masg*, F. M., the fortress of *Masg*, who was one of the ancestors of the Leinster people.

Dunamon, in Galway: so called from a castle of the same name on the Suck; but the name, which the annalists write *Dun-Iomgain*, Imgan's fort, was anciently applied to a *dun*, which is still partly preserved.

Dunboe, in Derry: the fortress of the cow.

Dunboyne, *Dun-Baeithin*, *Baeithin's* or Boyne's fort.

Duncannon, Conan's fortress.

Duncormick, Cormac's fortress.

Dundalk. The name was originally applied to the great fortress now called the moat of Castletown, a mile inland, which was the residence of *Cuchullin*, chief of the Red Branch knights in the first century. *Dun-Deal-gan* (Dalgan), F. M., the fortress of *Delga*, a Firbolg chief, who built it.

Dunderrow, in Cork: written *Dun-dermaigi* (Dundarwah) in the Book of Leinster, the fortress of the oak-plain (see Durrow); and the large dun from which it received the name is still in existence, half a mile south of the village.

Dundonald, in Down, Donall's fortress: so called from a fort that stands not far from the church.

Dundrum, *Dun-droma,* F. M., the fortress on the ridge or hill.

Duneane, in Antrim: written in the Felire of Aengus, *Dun-da-én* (Dun-a-ain), the fortress of the two birds.

Dunfanaghy, *Dun-Fionnchon* (Finahan), *Finchu's* fort.

Dungannon, in Tyrone: *Dun-Geanainn* (Gannin), F. M., *Geanan's* or Gannon's fortress.

Dungarvan, *Dun-Garbhain,* F. M., Garvan's fortress.

Dunhill, *Dun-aille,* the fortress of the cliff.

Dunkineely, in Donegal: *Dun-mhic-Chionnfhaelaidh* (Dunvickaneely), Mackineely's fort.

Dunkit, *Ceat's* or Keth's fortress.

Dunleer, in Louth. Old name *Land-léri* (Book of Leinster), the church (*land* or *lann*) of austerity. Present name formed by substituting *dun* a fort for *lann.*

Dunluce castle, near the Giant's Causeway: *Dunlios,* F. M., strong *lios* or fort. *Dun* is here an adjective, meaning strong.

Dunmanway, in Cork. Old name *Dun-na-mbeann* (Dun-aman), F. M., the fortress of the gables or pinnacles. The last syllable *way* is from *buidhe* yellow (bwee, or with the *b* aspirated, wee):—Dunmanway, the fortress of the yellow pinnacles.

Dunmore, great fort.

Dunmurry, *Dun-Muireadhaigh,* Murray's fort.

Dunquin, in Kerry: *Dun-caein* (Dunkeen), F. M., beautiful fort.

Dunshaughlin, in Meath. A church was founded here for bishop *Sechnall* or Secundinus, St. Patrick's nephew; and hence it was called *Domhnach-Seachnaill* (Donna-Shaughnill), F. M., the church of St. *Sechnall,* which has been shortened to the present name.

Duntryleague, in Limerick. According to a passage in the Book of Lismore, a *dun* or palace was built here for Cormac Cas, son of Olioll Olum (*see* Connello); and his bed was supported by three *liagáns* or pillar stones, from which the place was called *Dun-tri-liag*, the fortress of the three *liags* or pillar stones.

Durrow, in King's County, a favourite residence of St. Columbkille. Venerable Bede has a short passage in his Eccl. Hist. (lib. iii., cap. iv.), in which the original form and translation of this name are given:—"Before he (Columba) passed over into Britain, he had built a noble monastery in Ireland, which, from the great number of oaks, is in the Scotic (Irish) language called *Dearmhagh* (Darwah), the field of the oaks" (*dair* and *magh*).

Dysart (also Dysert), *see* Desert.

Dysartenos, in Queen's County. St. Aengus the Culdee, who died in the year 824, built a cell for himself here; and hence the place was called *Disert-Aenghusa*, Aengus's hermitage.

Easky, in Sligo: from the river:*Iascach* (Eeska), fishy (from *iasg*, a fish).

Eden, *Eudan* (edan), the brow; a hill brow.

Edenderry, the hill brow of the oak wood.

Edenmore, great hill brow.

Edergole (also Edergoole), *see* Addergoole.

Eglish, a church: *see* Aglish.

Eighter, *Iochtar* (eeter), lower.

Eliogarty, in Tipperary: a shortened form of Ely O'Fogarty (shortened by having the *f* aspirated and omitted: *see* p0), O'Fogarty's *Ely*, so called from its ancient possessors the O'Fogartys. *See* Ely.

Elphin, in Roscommon. St. Patrick founded a church here near a spring, over which stood a large stone; and hence the place was called *Aill-finn*, which Colgan interprets the rock (*aill*) of the clear spring (*finn* white, clear).

Ely. The different tribes called *Eile* or Ely were so named from their ancestor *Eile*, the seventh in descent from *Cian*, son of Olioll Olum (*see* Connello).

Emlagh, *Imleach* (Imlagh), land bordering on a lake; and hence a marshy or swampy place.

Emly, in Tipperary. St. *Ailbhe* founded his establishment here in the fifth century, on the margin of a lake, which has been only lately drained. The place is called in the Irish authorities *Imleach-iobhair* (yure), the lake-marsh of the yew tree.

Emlygrennan, in Limerick: a corruption of the Irish name *Bile-Ghroidhnín* (Billa-Gryneen), Grynan's ancient tree.

Enagh, the name of twenty townlands. Sometimes *Aenach*, a fair; sometimes *Eanach*, a marsh.

Ennereilly, in Wicklow: *Inbher-Daeile* (Invereela), F. M., the *inver* or mouth of the river formerly called the Deel, now the Pennycomequick.

Ennis, *inis,* an island; a meadow along a river.

Enniskeen, *Inis-caein* (keen), F. M., beautiful island or river meadow.

Enniskerry, *Ath-na-scairbhe* (Annascarvy), the ford of the *scarriff* or rough river-crossing; from an ancient stony ford where the old road crosses the river.

Enniskillen, *Inis-Cethlenn* (Kehlen), F. M., the island of *Kethlenn,* wife of Balor, the Fomorian king of Tory Island.

Ennistimon, *Inis-Diomain,* F. M., *Diaman's* river meadow.

Errigal, *Aireagal,* a habitation, a small church.

Errigal Keeroge, in Tyrone: *Aireagal Dachiarog* (Dakeeroge), F. M., the church of St. *Dachiarog.*

Errigal Trough, in Monaghan: the church of (the barony of) Trough.

Esker, *Eiscir,* a sandhill.

Eskeragh (also Eskragh), a place full of *eskers.*

Ess (also Essan, Essaun), a waterfall.

Estersnow, in Roscommon: a strange corruption from the Irish *Disert-Nuadhan* (Nooan), F. M., the hermitage of *St. Nuadha* (Nooa). Disert is often corrupted to *ister, ester, tirs, tristle,* etc.

Faddan, *Feadan,* a small brook.

Faha (also Fahy), an exercise green. *See* Faithche in vocabulary.

Farnagh (also Farnane, Farnoge), a place of *Fearns* (Farns), or alders.

Farney, in Monaghan: *Fearnmhagh* (Farnvah), Book of R., the alder plain (*fearn* and *magh*).

Farran, *Fearann,* land.

Farset (also Farsid), *Fearsad,* a sandbank in a river.

Fartagh (also Fertagh), a place of graves (*feart*).

Fasagh (also Fassagh), a wilderness (*Fásach*).

Fassadinin, in Kilkenny: the *fasagh* or wilderness of, or near, the river Dinin.

Feagh, *Fiodhach* (Feeagh), a woody place (*fidh*).

Fearmore, great grass (*féur*) or grassy place.

Feddan, *see* Faddan.

Feenagh, *Fiodhnach* (Feenagh), woody (*fidh*); a woody place.

Feighcullen, in Kildare: *Fiodh-Chuilinn,* F. M., Cullen's wood.

Fenagh, *see* Feenagh.

Fennor, *Fionnabhair* (Finner), F. M., white field.

Fermanagh, so called from the tribe of *Fir-monach,* O'Dugan), the men of *Monach,* who were originally a Leinster tribe, so named from their ancestor, *Monach,* fifth in descent from Cahirmore, monarch of Ireland from AD 120 to 123.

Fermoy, in Cork: *Feara-muighe* (Farra-moy), O'Dugan, the men of the plain.

Fermoyle, *Formaeil*, a round hill.

Fernagh (also Ferney), *see* Farnagh.

Ferns, *Fearna* (Farna), F. M., alders, a place abounding in alders: English plural termination added.

Ferrard, barony of, in Louth: *Feara-arda* (Farra-arda), F. M., the men of the height, i. e. of Slieve Bregh.

Fethard, *Fiodh-ard* (Fecard), F. M., high wood.

Fews, baronies of, in Armagh: *Feadha* (Fa), F. M., woods; with the English plural termination added. Fews in Waterford has the same origin.

Fiddan, (also Fiddane, Fiddaun), *see* Faddan.

Fiddown, in Kilkenny: *Fidh-duin* (Feedoon), F. M., the wood of the *dun* or fort.

Fingall, a district lying north of Dublin, in which the Danes settled; and hence it was called *Fine-Gall* (O'C. Cal.), the territory or tribe (*fine*) of the *Galls* or foreigners.

Finglas, clear stream (*fionn*, white, clear; and *glaise*).

Finn river and lake in Donegal: *Loch-Finne*, the lake of *Finna*, a woman, about whom there is an interesting legend. The river took its name from the lake. *See* Origin and History of Irish Names of Places, p 167.

Finnea, in Westmeath: *Fidh-an-atha* (Fee-an-aha) F. M., the wood of the ford.

Fintona, *Fionn-tamhnach* (Fintowna), F. M., fair coloured field.

Foil, *Faill*, a cliff.

Foilduff, black cliff.

Forenaght (also Forenaghts, Fornaght, Farnaght), *Fornocht*, a bare, naked, or exposed hill.

Formil (also Formoyle, Formweel), *see* Fermoyle.

Forth. The descendants of Ohy Finn *Fothart* (Fohart), brother of Conn of the hundred battles (king of Ireland from AD 123 to 158) were called *Fotharta* (Foharta), Book of R. Some of them settled in the present counties of Wexford and Carlow, where the two baronies of Forth still retain their name.

Foy (Foygh), forms of *Faithche. See* Faha.

Foybeg (also Foymore), little and great exercise green.

Foyduff, black exercise green.

Foyle, *see* Foil.

Freagh (also Freugh), *Fraech*, heath, a heathy place.

Freaghduff (also Freeduff), black heath.

Freaghillan (also Freaghillaun), heathy island (*oileán*).

Freshford, Irish name *Achadh-úr* (Book of Leinster), which should have been translated *Freshfield: Achadh* was mistaken for *ath.*

Freughmore (also Freaghmore), great heath.

Funcheon, *Fuinnseann* (Funshin), the ash tree: the ash-producing river.

Funshin (also Funshinagh, Funshog, Funshoge), a place producing ash trees (*fuinnse*).

Galbally (also Gallavally, Galvally, Galwally), English town; *Gall* here means an Englishman.

Galboley (also Galboola, Galbooley, Galwolie), a *booley* or dairy place belonging to *Galls* or English people.

Gallagh, a place full of rocks or standing stones. *See* Gall in vocabulary.

Gallan (also Gallane), *Gallan*, a standing stone.

Gallen. The descendants of *Cormac Gaileng*, great grandson of Olioll Olum (*see* Connello), were called *Gailenga* (O'Dugan), the race of Gaileng, and they gave name to the barony of Gallen in Mayo.

Gallon is used in Cavan to signify a measure of land.

Gallow, *see* Gallagh.

Gardrum (also Gargrim), *Gearr-dhruim*, short ridge or hill: *d* changed to *g* in Gargrim (*see* p. 7.).

Garnavilla, in Tipperary: *Garran-a'-bhile* (Garranavilla), the shrubbery of the *bile* or old tree.

Garracloon, *Garbh-chluain*, rough meadow.

Garran (also Garrane, Garraun), *Garrán*, a shrubbery.

Garranamanagh, the shrubbery of the monks (*manach*).

Garranbane (also Garranbaun), white shrubbery.

Garranekinnefeake, Kinnefeake's shrubbery.

Garry, a garden (*garradha*).

Garryard, high garden.

Garrycastle. The Mac Coghlans' castle, near Banagher in King's County, is called in the annals *Garrdha-an-chaislein* (Garrancashlane), the garden of the castle; and from this the modern name Garrycastle has been formed, and extended to the barony.

Garryduff, black garden (*dubh*).

Garrymore, great garden.

Garryowen, near Limerick: Owen's garden.

Garrysallagh, dirty garden (*salach*).

Garryspellane, Spellane's garden.

Gartan, a little garden. *See* Gort in vocabulary.

Garvagh, *Garbhach*, rough land (from *garbh*, rough).

Garvaghy, rough *achadh* or field.

Garvary, *Garbhaire*, rough land.

Gay island in Fermanagh, goose island (*gedh*).

Geara (also Gearagh, Gairha), *Gaertha* (gairha) a bush place along a river.

Gearhameen river, at Killarney: *min* smooth, small; a *gearha* composed of small delicate bushes.

Giants' Causeway. Irish name *Clochán-na-bhFomharaigh*

(Clohanavowry), the *cloghan* or stepping stones of the Fomorians. These sea rovers were magnified into giants in popular legend, and the name came to be translated 'Giants' Causeway.'

Girley, in Meath: *Greallach* (Grallagh), a miry place.

Glack, *Glaic,* a hollow.

Glanbehy, birchy glen (*beith*).

Glantane (also Glantaun), little glen.

Glanworth, in Cork: recently corrupted from its Irish name, *Gleann-amhnach* (Glenounagh), as it is written in the Book of Rights, the watery or marshy glen.

Glascloon, green *cloon* or meadow.

Glasdrummon (also Glasdrummond), green ridge.

Glashaboy (also Glashawee), yellow streamlet (*glaise* and *buidhe*).

Glasheen, a little stream.

Glasmullagh, green *mullach* or summit.

Glasnevin, near Dublin: takes name from a streamlet flowing through Delville into the Tolka at the bridge. In remote ages some pagan chief named *Naeidhe* (Nee), must have resided on its banks; from him it was called *Glas-Naeidhen* (Neean), F. M., *Naeidhe's* streamlet; and the name extended to the village, while its original application is quite forgotten.

Glassan, a green place.

Glasthule, *Glas-Tuathail* (thoohil), *Tuathal's* or Toole's streamlet.

Glenagarey, *Gleann-na-gcaerach* (Glenagaira), the glen of the sheep (*caera*).

Glenanair, the glen of slaughter (*ár*).

Glenavy, in Antrim. The *G* is a modern addition. The Irish name, as given in the Calendar, is *Lann-Abhaich* (Lanavy), the church of the dwarf. When St. Patrick had built the church there, he left it in charge of his disciple Daniel, who, from his low stature, was called *Abhac* (avak or ouk), i. e. dwarf.

Glenbane (also Glenbaun), white glen.

Glencar, on the borders of Leitrim and Sligo: *Gleann-a'-chairthe* (Glenacarha), the glen of the pillar stone (*cairthe*).

Glencullen (also Glencullin), holly glen (*cuillionn*).

Glendine (also Glandine), deep glen (*doimhin*).

Glendowan mountains, in Donegal: *see* Glendine.

Glenduff, black glen (*dubh*).

Glengarriff, rough or rugged glen (*garbh*).

Gleninagh, ivy glen (see *eidhneán* in vocabulary).

Glenkeen, beautiful glen.

Glenmore, great glen.

Glennamaddy, the valley of the dogs (ṁ*adadh*).

Glenogra, in Limerick: Ogra's glen.

Glenosheen, in Limerick: *Oisin's* or Osheen's glen.

Glenquin, barony of, in Limerick: *see* p 7.

Glenreagh (also Glenrevagh), grey glen.

Glenroe, red glen (*ruadh*).

Glentane (also Glentaun), little glen.

Glenties, in Donegal: *Gleanntaidhe* (glenty), glens; from two fine glens at the head of which it stands.

Glenwhirry, in Antrim: *Gleann-a'-choire* (Glenacurry: change of *ch* to *wh*), the glen of the river Curry or *Coire*. *Coire* means a caldron, and the river got this name from a deep pool formed under a cataract.

Glynn, a glen or valley.

Gneeve (also Gneeves), *Gniomh* (gneeve), a measure of land.

Gola, forks; the plural of *gabhal* (goul).

Golan, a little *goul* or fork.

Golden, in Tipperary: *Gabhailin* (Gouleen), a little fork: the Suir divides there for a short distance, forming a fork.

Gort, *Gort*, a tilled field.

Gortahork (also Gortahurk), the field of the oats (*coirce*).

Gortalassa, the field of the *lis* or fort.

Gortanure (also Gortinure), the field of the yew.

Gortavoher, the field of the *boher* or road.

Gortboy, yellow field (*buidhe*).

Gortbrack, speckled field (*breac*).

Gorteen, little field.

Gortfad *(also* Gortfadda), long field.

Gortgranagh, grain field.

Gortin, little field; *see* Gorteen.

Gortmore, great field.

Gortnaglogh, *Gort-na-gcloch*, the field of the stones.

Gortnagross, *Gort-na-gcros*, the field of the crosses.

Gortnahoo (also Gortnahoon), the field of the cave (*uaimh).*

Gortnamona, the field of the bog (*moin*).

Gortnamucklagh, the field of the piggeries. *See* Mucklagh.

Gortnasillagh, the field of the sallows.

Gortnaskea (also Gortnaskeagh, Gortnaskeha, Gortnaskey), the field of the *sceachs* or whitethorn bushes.

Gortreagh, grey field (*riabhach*).

Gortroe, red field (*ruadh*).

Gougane Barra, in Cork: St. Finbar's rock-cleft.

Goul (also Gowel), *Gabhal*, a fork.

Gowlan (also Gowlane, Gowlaun), little fork.

Graffa (also Graffin, Graffoge, Graffy), grubbed land, or land rooted up by a *grafaun* or grubbing axe.

Graigue, a village.

Graiguenamanagh, the village of the monks.

Grallagh, *Greallach* (Grallagh), a miry place.

Granagh (also Granaghan), a place producing grain.

Grangegeeth, windy grange (*gaeth*).

Gransha, a grange, a place for grain.

Greagh, a moory level spot among hills.

Great Connell, great *congbhail* or habitation (*see* Conwal).

Greenan (also Greenane, Greenaun, Grenan), *Grianan*, a summer residence, a royal palace. From *grian*, the sun.

Greenoge, a sunny little spot. From *grian*.

Grillagh (also Grellagh), *see Grallagh.*

Gurteen, little tilled field; *see Gorteen.*

Gurteenroe, red little field.

Guilcagh, a place producing broom (*giolcach*, broom).

Gyleen, near Trabolgan in Cork: little *gobhal* or fork.

Heagles, near Ballymoney: *Eaglais*, a church.

Howth, from the Danish *Hoved*, a head. Old Irish name *Ben Edar*, the peak of Edar, a legendary personage.

Idrone, baronies of, in Carlow. So called from the tribe of *Hy Drona* (Book of R.), the former occupants, who were named from their ancestor *Drona*, fourth in descent from Cahirmore, monarch of Ireland from AD 120 to 123.

Illan (also Illane, Illaun), *Oileán* (oilaun), an island.

Imaile, in Wicklow: *Hy Mail* (O'Dugan), the descendants of Mann *Mal*, brother of Cahirmore. See Idrone.

Inch, *Inis*, an island; a low meadow along a river.

Inchmore, great island or river meadow.

Inis (also Inish), an island.

Inishannon, in Cork: written in the Book of Leinster *Inis-Eoganain* (Inishowenan), Owenan's or little Owen's island or river meadow.

Inishargy, in Down: called in the Taxation of 1306, *Inyscargi*, showing that the Irish form is *Inis-carraige*, the island of the rock. The rising ground where the church stands was formerly surrounded by marshes.

Inishbofin, the island of the white cow (*bo*): name explained by a legend.

Inishkeen, beautiful island.

Inishkeeragh, the island of sheep (*caera*).

Inishlounaght, in Tipperary: *Inis-leamhnachta* (lounaghta), the island or river holm of the new milk, probably because it was good grazing land.

Inishmaan (also Inishmean), middle island (*meadhon*).

Inishmacsaint, a parish in Fermanagh, taking its name from an island in Lough Erne, which is called in the annals *Inis-muighe-samh* (moy-sauv), the island of the plain of sorrel, from which the present name has been formed by a corrupt pronunciation.

Inishmore, great island.

Inishowen, in Donegal: the island of Owen, son of Niall of the Nine Hostages (king from 379 to 405). *See* Tyrone.

Inishrush, the island of the peninsula (*ros*).

Inishturk, in Mayo: *Inis-tuirc,* Hy F., the boar's island (*torc*). Several islands of this name.

Inishtioge, in Kilkenny: written in the Book of Leinster *Inis-Teoc, Teoc's* island.

Innisfallen, in the lower Lake of Killarney: called in the Book of Leinster *Inis-Faithlenn* (Fahlen), the island of *Faithlenn,* a man's name.

Inver, *Inbhear* (inver), the mouth of a river.

Ireland's Eye. Original name *Inis-Ereann* (Eran) (the island of *Eire* or Eria, a woman), of which the present name is an attempted translation. *Eye* is the Danish *ey,* an island, and the translators understanding *Ereann* to mean Ireland, rendered the name Ireland's *Ey* (or island) instead of Eria's *Ey.* (*See* Origin and History of Irish Names of Places, pp. 76, 101, 104.)

Isertkelly, in Galway: corrupted (similarly to the next two names) from *Diseart-Cheallaigh* (Disertkelly), F. M., *Cellach's* or Kelly's hermitage.

Isertkieran, in Tipperary: the *desert* or hermitage of St. Kieran of Ossory. *See* Seirkieran.

Ishartmon, in Wexford: the *desert* or hermitage of St. Munna.*See* Taghmon.

Island Magee, the island or peninsula of the *Mac Aedhas* or Magees, its former possessors. Anciently called *Rinn-Seimhne* (Rinn-sevne), the point of *Seimhne,* the old territory in which it was situated.

Iverleary, in Cork: took its name from the O'Leary, its ancient proprietors. *See* next name.

Iverk, in Kilkenny: *Ui-Eirc (Ee-erc),* O'Dugan, a tribe name, signifying the descendants of *Erc. Ui* (ee) or *uibh* (iv), signifies descendants.

Iveruss, in Limerick: the old tribe of *Uibh-Rosa* the descendants of *Rosa.*

Kanturk, in Cork: *Ceann-tuirc* (Kanturk), F. M., the boar's head or hill; from the hill near the town.

Keadew (also Keady), *Ceide* (Keady), a hill level and smooth at top.

Keale (also Keel), *Caol,* narrow; a narrow place, valley, or river.

Keeloge (also Keeloges), Caelóg, a narrow stripe or ridge.

Keelty, *Coillte* (Coiltha), woods, from *coill.*

Keenagh (also Keenaghan), a mossy place (*caenach,* moss).

Keenaght barony in Londonderry. The descendants of *Cian* (Kean), son of Olioll Olum (*see* Connello), were called *Cianachta* (Keenaghta), i. e. the race of *Cian*. The O'Conors of Glengiven, who were a portion of this tribe, possessed the barony of Keenaght, and gave it its name.

Keimaneigh, pass of, in Cork: *Ceim-an-fhiaigh* (Kamean-ee), the pass of the deer (*fiadh*).

Kenmare, *Ceann-mara,* the head of the sea (*muir*), i.e. the highest point reached by the tide in a river. *See* Kinvarra and Kinsale.

Kerry. The descendants of *Ciar* (Keer: *see* Connemara) were called *Ciarraidhe* (Keery: Book of R.), i. e. the race of *Ciar*. They possessed the territory lying west of Abbeyfeale, which was called from them *Ciarraighe*, and ultimately gave name to the whole county.

Kesh, in Fermanagh: *Ceis* (Kesh), a wickerwork causeway.

Keshcarrigan, in Leitrim: the wickerwork causeway of the little rock.

Kilbaha, *Coill-beithe,* birch wood.

Kilbarron, in Donegal: St. Barron's church.

Kilbarry, in Waterford and Cork: from St. Finbar. *See* Cork and Gougane Barra.

Kilbeg, small church or wood.

Kilbeggan, Beccan's church.

Kilbeheny, *Coill-beithne* (Kilbehena), F. M., birch wood.

Kilbreedy, *Cill-Bhrighde,* St. Brigid's church.

Kilbride, *see* Kilbreedy.

Kilbroney, church of *Bronagh,* a virgin saint.

Kilcarragh, in Kerry and Waterford: the church of St. *Carthach* (Caurha) of Lismore.

Kilcavan, in Wexford: church dedicated to St. Kevin of Glendalough.

Kilcleagh (also Kilclay), *see* Kilclief.

Kilclief, in Down: *Cill-cleithe* (Kilcleha), the hurdle church (*cliath*). The original church was constructed of hurdles, after the early Irish fashion.

Kilcolman, St. Colman's church.

Kilcommon, St. Coman's church.

Kilcullen, *Cill-cuillinn,* the church of the holly.

Kildalkey, in Meath: written in an Irish charter in the Book of Kells, *Cill-Delga,* Delga's church.

Kildare. According to Animosus, St. Brigid built her little cell here under a very high oak tree, and hence it was called *Cill-dara,* which the same writer translates *Cella quercus,* the cell or church of the oak.

Kildimo, in Limerick: St. Dima's church.

Kildorrery, in Cork: *Cill-dairbhre* (Kildarrery), the church of the oaks. *See* Darraragh.

Doorway, round tower near Kildare

Kildrought, in Kildare. *See* Celbridge.

Kilduff, black church or wood.

Kilfinnane, in Limerick: the church of St. Finan. *See* Ardfinnan.

Kilfithmone, in Tipperary: the church of the wood of the bog (*fidh* and *móin*).

Kilflyn, Flann's church.

Kilgarriff (also Kilgarve), rough wood.

Kilgarvan, *St. Garbhan's* or Garvan's church.

Kilkee, in Clare: St. *Caeidhe's* (Kee's) church.

Kilkeedy, in Clare and Limerick: St. *Caeide's* (Keedy's) church.

Kilkeel, narrow church.

Kilkenny, *Cill-Chainnigh* (Kilkenny), F.M., the church of St. *Cainneach,* or Canice, who died in the year 598. *See* Aghaboe.

Killadysart, the church of the *desert* or hermitage

Killaloe, in Clare and Kilkenny: *Cill-Dalua* (Killaloo. *d* aspirated—*see* p 5), the church of St. Dalua or Molua, who flourished in the sixth century.

Killanummery, in Leitrim: *Cill-an-iomaire* (ummera), F.M., the church of the ridge.

Killarney, *Cill-airne*, the church of the sloes.

Killashandra. The original church was built within the enclosure of a rath or fort which still partly exists, hence *Cill-a'-sean-ratha* (Killashanraha), the church of the old rath.

Killashee, in Kildare: *Cill-ausaille*, the church of St. *Ausaille* or Auxilius, a contemporary of St. Patrick. Killashee in Longford is probably the church of the *sidh* or fairy hill.

Killaspugbrone, near Sligo. In the Book of Armagh it is stated that St. Patrick built a church at *Cassel Irra* for his disciple *Brón* or Bronus, who became bishop of *Cuil Irra*, the peninsula lying south-west of Sligo: hence the place was called *Cill-easpuig-Bróin*, F. M., the church of bishop Bronus (*easpug*, a bishop).

Killaspuglonane, in Clare: *Cill-easpuig-Fhlannáin*, F. M., the church of bishop Flannan.

Killawillin, in Cork: *Cill-a'-mhuilinn*, the church of the mill.

Killeany, in Clare and Galway: the church of St. Eany or Endeus of Aran, who flourished in the fifth century.

Killeedy, in Limerick: the church of the virgin saint Ita or *Ide*, who founded a nunnery here in the early part of the sixth century. *See* Kilmeedy.

Killeen, the name of more than 80 townlands, nearly all from *Cillín* a little church, but a few from *Coillín*, a little wood.

Killeentierna, in Kerry: *Tighernach's* (Tierna's) little church.

Killeigh, in King's County: *Cill-achaidh* (Killahy), F. M., the church of the field.

Killenaule, in Tipperary: the church of St. *Naile* (Nawly) or Natalis.

Killery harbour, in Connemara: corrupted by a change of *l* to *r* (*see* p 6), from *Cael-shaile* (Keelhaly), narrow sea-inlet, but the full name is *Cael-shaile-ruadh*, F. M., the reddish (*ruadh*) narrow sea-inlet.

Killevy (also Killeavy), in Armagh: called from its proximity to Slieve Gullion, *Cill-shleibhe* (Killeva), F. M., the church of the *sliabh* or mountain.

Killiney, in Dublin: corrupted from *Cill-inghen* (Killineen); full name *Cill-inghen-Leinín*, the church of the daughters of *Leinin*.

Killiney, in Kerry: *see* Killeany.

Killisk (also Killiskey), the church of the water (*uisge*).

Killoe, *Cill-eó*, O'C. Cal., the church of the yews.

Killure, *Cill-iubhair*, the church of the yew.

Killursa, *Cili-Fhursa*, the church of St. Fursa, who flourished in the sixth century.

Killybegs, *Cealla-beaga,* F. M., little churches.

Killygorden, in Donegal: *Coill-na-gcuiridin* (Kilnagur-ridin), F. M., the wood of the parsnips.

Killyon, the church of St. *Liadhan* (Leean) or Liedania, mother of St. *Ciaran* of Ossory. *See* Seirkieran.

Kilmacanoge, in Wicklow: the church of St. *Mochonog,* one of the primitive Irish saints.

Kilmacrenan, in Donegal: *see* p 7.

Kilmainham, near Dublin: *see* p 7.

Kilmallock, in Limerick: *Cill-Mocheallog* (Kilmohelog), the church of St. *Mocheallog,* who flourished in the beginning of the seventh century.

Kilmanagh, near Kilkenny: *Cill-manach* (Mart. Taml.), the church of the monks.

Kilmeedy, the church of St. *Mide,* or Ité, for both are the same name. *See* Killeedy.

Kilmihil, the church of St. Michael the Archangel.

Kilmore, there are about 80 parishes and townlands of this name, most of them signifying great church, some great wood (*cill* and *coill*).

Kilmurry. There are more than fifty places of this name, which were all so called from places dedicated to the Blessed Virgin: *Cill-Mhuire,* Mary's church.

Kilnaleck, the wood of the flag-surfaced land.

Kilnamanagh, in Tipperary: *Coill-na-manach,* F. M., the wood of the monks.

Kilnamona, the church of the bog (*moin*).

Kilpatrick, St. Patrick's church.

Kilquane, *Cill-Chuain,* St. Cuan's church.

Kilrook, in Antrim: *Cill-ruadh,* F. M., red church.

Kilrush, the church of the wood or peninsula.

Kilskeer, in Meath: the church of the virgin saint *Scire,* who flourished in the sixth century.

Kiltenanlea, in Clare: *Cill-tSenain-leith,* the church of St. Senan the hoary.

Kiltullagh, in Roscommon: *Cill-tulaigh,* the church of the hill.

Kiltwbegs, *Coillte-beaga,* little woods.

Kilwatermoy, in Waterford: *water* is here a corruption of *uachtar,* upper: the church of the upper plain.

Kinalea, barony of, in Cork: *Cinel-Aedha* (Kinel-Ay), O'Dugan, the descendants of *Aedh* or Hugh, who was the father of *Failbhe-Flann,* king of Munster in A D 636.

Kinalmeaky, barony of, in Cork: *Cinel-mBece* (Kinel-mecka), O'Dugan, the descendants of *Bece,* the ancestor of the O'Mahonys.

Kinard, *Ceann-ard,* high head or hill.

Kinawley, in Fermanagh: *Cill-Naile* (Kilnawly, which would have been the correct anglicised form), O'C. Cal., the church of St. *Naile* or Natalis, who died in A D 564.

Kincon, the hound's head (*ceann* and *cu*).

Kincora, at Killaloe, the site of Brian Boru's palace, took its name from an ancient weir across the Shannon: *Ceann-coradh* (Kancora), F. M., the head or hill of the weir.

Kinneigh (also Kinnea), *Ceann-ech*, F. M., the horse's head or hill.

Kinnitty, in King's County: *Ceann-Eitigh* (Kan-Etty), *Etech's* head. So called, according to a gloss in the Felire of Aengus, because the head of *Etech*, an ancient Irish princess, was buried there.

Kinsale (also Kinsaley),*Ceann-saile*, the head of the brine, i. e. the highest point to which the tide rises in a river. *See* Kenmare.

Kinure, *Ceann-uibhair*, the head of the yew.

Kinvarra, in Galway: *Ceann-mhara*, F. M., the head of the sea. *See* Kenmare.

Knappagh, *Cnapach*, a place full of *cnaps* or round hillocks.

Knock, *Cnoc*, a hill.

Knockacullen, the hill of the holly.

Knockaderry, the hill of the oak wood.

Knockagh, *Cnocach*, a hilly place.

Knockainy, in Limerick: the hill of *Aine* or Ainy, a celebrated *banshee.*

Knockalisheen, the hill of the little *lis* or fort.

Knockalough, the hill of the lake.

Knockane (also Knockaun), little hill.

Knockanglass (also Knockaneglass), green little hill.

Knockanree, *see* p 5.

Knockanroe (Knockaneroe, Knockaunroe), red little hill.

Knockanure, *Cnoc-aniubhair*, yew hill.

Knockatemple, the hill of the temple or church.

Knockatirriv (also Knockatarry, Knockaterriff), *Cnoc-a'-tairbh*, the hill of the bull.

Knockatober, the hill of the well.

Knockatoor, the hill of the *tuar* or bleach green.

Knockatotaun, *Cnoc-a'-teotain*, the hill of the burning or conflagration.

Knockaunbaun, white little hill.

Knockavilla (also Knockaville), the hill of the *bile* or old tree.

Knockavoe, near Strabane: *Cnock-Buidhbh* (Knockboov), F. M., the hill of Bove Derg, a legendary Tuatha De Danann chief.

Knockbane (also Knockbaun), white hill.

Knockboy, *Cnoc-buidhe*, yellow hill.

Knockbrack, *Cnoc-breac*, speckled hill.

Knockcroghery, in Roscommon: the hill of the *crochaire* or hangman. It was a place of execution.

Knockdoo (also Knockduff), *see* p 5.

Knockeen, little hill.

Knockfierna, in Limerick: *Cnoc-fírinne*, the hill of truth, or of truthful prediction, for it serves as a *weather glass* to the people of the circumjacent plains, who can predict whether the day will be wet or dry by the appparance of the summit in the morning.

Knockglass, *Cnoc-glas*, green hill.

Knockgorm, *Cnoc-gorm*, blue hill.

Knocklayd, in Antrim: called from its shape *Cnoc-leithid* (lehid), the hill of breadth, i. e. broad hill.

Knocklofty, in Tipperary: *Cnoc-lochta*, the *lofted* or shelving hill.

Knocklong, in Limerick: *Cnoc-luinge*, the hill of the encampment, for Cormac mac Art encamped with his army, on this hill, when he invaded Munster in the third century.

Knockmanagh, middle hill.

Knockmealdown mountains, *Cnoc-Maeldomhnaigh*, Maeldowney's hill.

Knockmore, great hill.

Knockmoyle, *Cnoc-mael*, bald or bare hill.

Knockmullin, the hill of the mill.

Knocknaboley (also Knocknabooly), the hill of the *booley* or dairy place.

Knocknacrohy, *Cnoc-na-croiche*, the hill of the gallows; a place of execution.

Knocknagapple (also Knocknagappul), *Cnoc na-gcapall*, the hill of the horses.

Knocknagaul, in Limerick: the hill of the *Galls* or foreigners.

Knocknageeha, the hill of the wind (*gaeth*).

Knocknagin, *Cnoc-na-gceann* (na-gan), the hill of the heads; a place of execution.

Knocknaglogh, the hill of the stones (*cloch*).

Knocknagore, the hill of the goats (*gabhar*).

Knocknahorna, the hill of the barley (*eórna*).

Knocknamona, the hill of the bog.

Knocknamuck, the hill of the pigs.

Knocknarea, in Sligo: the hill of the executions. *See* Ardnarea.

Knocknaskagh (also Knocknaskeagh), the hill of the *sceachs* or white thorn bushes.

Knockninny, a hill in Fermanagh, which gives name to a barony, *Cnoc-Ninnidh* (Ninny), the hill of St. *Ninnidh*, who was a contemporary of St. Columba.

Knockpatrick, Patrick's hill.

Knockraha, (also Knockrath, Knocknaraha), the hill of the *rath* or fort.

Knockranny, *Cnoc-raithnigh* (rahnee), ferny hill.

Knockrawer (also Knockramer, Knockrower, Knockrour), *Cnoc-reamhar* (rawer or rower), *fat* or thick hill.

Knockreagh, grey hill.

Knockroe, red hill.

Knockshanbally, the hill of the old town.

Knocksouna, near Kilmallock in Limerick: written in the Book of Lismore, *Cnoc-Samhna* (Souna), the hill of *Samhuin* (Sowan or Savin), the first of November, which was kept as a festival by the pagan Irish. *See* Origin and History of Irish Names of Places, p 194.

Knocktemple, the hill of the temple or church.

Knocktopher, in Kilkenny: *see* p 7.

Knoppoge (also Knappoge), a little hill. *See* Knappagh.

Kyle, about half the names partly or wholly formed from Kyle, are from *Cill*, a church; the other half from *Coill*, a wood.

Kylebeg, small church or wood.

Kylemore, generally great wood (*coill*), sometimes great church (*cill*). Kylemore (lake) near the Twelve Pins in Connemara, is *Coill-mhor*, great wood.

Labby (also Labby), *Leaba* (labba), a bed, a grave.

Labbasheeda, in Clare: *Leaba-Sioda*, *Sioda's* or Sheedy's *labba*, bed, or grave.

Labbamolaga, St. Molaga's grave. *See* Templemolaga.

Lack, *leac* (lack), a stone, a flag stone.

Lacka, the side of a hill.

Lackabane (also Lackabaun), white hill side.

Lackagh, a place full of stones or flags.

Lackamore, great hill side.

Lackan, *see* Lacka.

Lackandarragh (also Lackendarragh), the hill side of the oaks.

Lackareagh, grey hill side (*riabhach*).

Lackaroe, red hill side (*ruadh*).

Lackeen, a little rock or flag.

Lacken, *see* Lacka.

Lag (also Legg), a hollow; a hollow in a hill.

Lagan, a little hollow. Sometimes it means a pillar stone (*liagan*). The river Lagan probably took its name from a little hollow on some part of its course.

Laghil (also Laghile), *Leamhchoill* (Lavwhill), elm wood.

Laght, *Leacht*, a sepulchre or monument.

Laghy, a slough, a miry place.

Laharan, *Leath-fhearann* (Laharan), half land.

Lahard, *Leath-ard*, half height; a gentle hill.

Lahardan (also Lahardane, Lahardaun), a gentle hill.

Lakyle, *Leath-choill*, half wood.

Lambay island near Dublin. The latter part is Danish: Lamb-ey, i. e. lamb island. Its ancient Irish name was

Rechru or *Reachra*; and the adjacent parish on the mainland was called from it, *Port-Reachrann* (Portrahern), the *port* or landing place of *Reachra*, which in the course of ages, has been softened down to the present name, Portraine.

Laragh (also Lauragh), *Lathrach*, the site of any thing.

Laraghbryan, in Kildare: Bryan's house site.

Largan, *Leargan*, the side or slope of a hill.

Largy, *Leargaidh, see* Largan.

Larne, in Antrim: *Latharna* (Laharna: Book of L.), the district of *Lathair* (Laher), son of Hugony the great, monarch of Ireland before the Christian era. Until recently it was the name of a district which extended northwards towards Glenarm, and the town was then called *Inver-an-Laharna*, the river mouth of (the territory of) Larne, from its situation at the mouth of the *Ollarbha* or Larne Water.

Latt, *see* Laght.

Latteragh, in Tipperary: *Leatracha* (Latraha), the plural of *Leitir*, a wet hill-side (*see* Letter). It is called in O'C. Cal., *Letracha-Odhrain* (Oran), *Odhran's* wet hill-slopes, from the patron, St. *Odhran*, who died in the year 548.

Laughil, *Leamhchoill* (Lavwhill), elm wood.

Laune river, at Killarney: *Leamhain*, F. M., elm; the elm-producing river.

Lavagh, *Leamhach* (Lavagh), a place producing elms.

Lavally, *Leath-bhaile*, half town or townland.

Lavey, in Cavan: *see* Lavagh.

Leagh, *Liath* (Leea), grey; a grey place.

Leam, *Leim*, a leap.

Leamlara, in Cork: the mare's leap.

Leamnamoyle, in Fermanagh: the leap of the *mael* or hornless cow.

Lear, *see* Lyre.

Lecale, barony of, in Down, *Leth-Chathail* (Lecahil), F. M., *Cathal's* half. *Cathal* was a chief who flourished about the year 700, and in a division of territory, this district was assigned to him, and took his name.

Lecarrow, *Leth-ceathramhadh* (Lecarhoo), half quarter (of land).

Leck, *see* Lack.

Leckan (also Leckaun), *see* Lacka.

Leckpatrick, Patrick's flag-stone.

Leeg (also Leek, Leeke), *see* Lack.

Legacurry (also Legaghory), *Lag-a-choire* (curry), the hollow (*lag*) of the caldron or pit.

Legan (also Legaun), *see* Lagan.

Legland, *see* Leighlin. *D* added: *see* p 7.

Lehinch, *Leith-innse*, F. M., half island, i. e. a peninsula.

Leighlin, in Carlow: *Leith-ghlionn* (Leh-lin), F. M., half glen; from some peculiarity of formation in the little river bed.

Leighmoney, grey *muine* or shrubbery.

Leinster. In the third century before the Christian era, *Labhradh Loingseach* (Lavra Linshagh, Lavra the mariner), brought an army of Gauls from France to assist him in recovering the kingdom from his uncle, the usurper, Coffagh Cael Bra. These foreign soldiers used a kind of broad pointed spear, called *laighen* (layen); and from this circumstance the province in which they settled, which had previously borne the name of *Galian*, was afterwards called *Laighen*, which is its present Irish name. The termination *ster*, which has been added to the names of three of the provinces, is the Scandinavian or Danish *stadr*, a place. *Laighen-ster* (the place or province of *Laighen*) would be pronounced *Laynster*, which is the very name given in a state paper of 1515, and which naturally settled into the present form, Leinster.

Leitrim, the name of more than 40 townlands and villages: *Laith-dhruim* (Lee-drum), F. M., grey *drum* or ridge.

Leixlip, a Danish name, meaning salmon leap (*lax*, a salmon), from the well-known cataract on the Liffey, still called Salmon leap, a little above the village. By Irish-Latin writers it is often called *Saltus-salmonis* (the leap of the salmon), and from this word *saltus*, a leap, the baronies of Salt in Kildare have taken their name.

Lemanaghan, in King's County: *Liath-Manchain*, F. M., St. Manchan's grey land.

Lena (also Leny), a wet meadow.

Lenamore, great wet meadow.

Lerrig, in Kerry: a hill side. *See* Largan.

Letter, *Leitir*, a wet hill side.

Lettera (also Letteragh, Lettery), wet hill-sides. *See* Latteragh.

Letterkenny, a shortened form of *Letter-Cannanan*, the O'Cannanans' hill-slope. The O'Cannanans, or as they now call themselves, Cannons, were anciently chiefs or kings of Tirconnell, till they ultimately sank under the power of the O'Donnells.

Lettermacaward, in Donegal: *Leitir-Mic-a'-bhaird*, the hill slope of Mac Ward, or the bard's son.

Lettermore, great wet hill-side.

Lettermullan, *Leitir-Meallain*, F. M., Meallan's hill-slope.

Levally, *see* Lavally.

Levny. The descendants of *Luigh* or Lewy, the son of *Cormac Gaileng* (*see* Gallen), were called *Luighne*

(Leyny: O'Dugan), and they gave name to the barony of Leyny in Sligo (*ne*, descendants).

Lick, *see* Lack.

Lickbla, in Westmeath: shortened from *Liag-Bladhma* (Leeg-Blawma), F. M., the flag-stone of *Bladh* (Blaw), a man's name. *See* Slieve Bloom.

Lickeen, little flag-stone.

Lickfinn, in Tipperary: white flag-stone.

Lickmolassy, in Galway: St. *Molaise's* (Molasha's) flag-stone.

Lickoran, the flag of the cold spring (*uaran*).

Limerick, corrupted from the Irish form *Luimnech* (Liminagh), F. M., by a change of *n* to *r* (*see* p 7): the name signifies a bare spot of land, from *lom*, bare.

Lis (also Liss), *Lios*, a circular earthen fort.

Lisalbanagh, the *Albanagh's* or Scotchman's fort.

Lisanisk (also Lisanisky), the fort of the water (*uisge*).

Lisbane (also Lisbaun), white *lis* or fort.

Lisbellaw, *Lios-bel-atha*, the *lis* of the ford-mouth.

Lisboy, yellow fort; probably from furze blossoms.

Liscannor, in Clare: Canar's fort.

Liscarrol, in Cork: *Cearbhall's* or Carroll's fort.

Liscartan, the fort of the forge (*ceardcha*).

Lisdoonvarna, in Clare: takes its name from a large fort on the right of the road as you go from Ballyvaghan to Ennistymon. The proper name of this is *Dunbhearnach* (Doonvarna), gapped fort (*see* Barna), from its shape, and the word *Lis* was added, somewhat in the same manner as 'river' in the expression 'the river Liffey': Lisdoonvarna, i. e. the *lis* (of) Doonvarna.

Lisdowney, in Kilkenny: Downey's fort.

Lisduff (also Lidsoo), *Lios-dubh*, black fort.

Lisheen, little *lis* or fort.

Lislea, *Lios-liath* (lee), grey fort.

Lislevane, in Cork: *Lios-leamhain*, elm fort.

Lismore, great fort. Lismore in Waterford received its name from the *lis* or entrenchment built by St. *Carthach* (Caurhagh) round his religious establishment. It was previously called *Magh-sciath* (Maskee), the plain of the shield. *See* Origin and History of Irish Names of Places, p 261.

Lismoyle, *Lios-mael*, bald or dilapidated fort.

Lismullin, the fort of the mill.

Lisnagat, *Lios-na-gcat*, the fort of the (wild) cats.

Lisnageeragh, the fort of the sheep (*caera*).

Lisnalee, the fort of the calves (*laegh*). *See* p 5.

Lisnamuck, the *lis* or fort of the pigs.

Lisnaskea, in Fermanagh: the fort of the *sceach* or white-thorn tree. It took its name from the celebrated *Sceach-ghabhra* (Skagowra), under which the Maguire used to be inaugurated.

Lisnisk (also Lisnisky), the fort of the water.

Lissan (also Lissane), little *lis* or fort.

Lissaniska (also Lissanisky), the fort of the water.

Lissaphuca, the fort of the *pooka* or spright.

Lissard, high fort.

Listowel, *Lios-Tuathail* (Lis-Thoohil), *Tuathal's* fort.

Lissonuffy, in Roscommon: *Lios-O-nDubhthaigh* (Liso-nuffy), F. M., the fort of the O'Duffys.

Lixnaw, in Kerry: *Lic-Snamha* (Snawa), F. M., the flag-stone of the swimming (*snamh*). *See* Drumsna.

Loughill (also Loughil), *Leamhchoill* (Lavwhill), elm wood.

Londonderry. Its most ancient name, according to all our authorities, was *Doire-Chalgaich* (Derry-Calgagh), the derry or oak wood of *Calgach* or *Galgacus*. In the tenth or eleventh century it began to be called *Derry-Columcille*, in honour of St. Columbkille, who founded his monastery there in 546, and this name continued to the time of James I, whose charter, granted to a company of London merchants, imposed the name of Londonderry.

Longfield, in almost all cases a corruption of *Leamh-choill* (Lavwhill), elm wood.

Longford, *Longphort* (Longfort), a fortress. The town of Longford is called in the Annals Longford O'Farrell, from a castle of the O'Farrells, the ancient proprietors.

Loop Head, in Clare: a Danish modification of Leap Head; Irish *Leim-Chonchuillinn* (Leam-Conhullin), F. M., *Cuchullin's* leap. For legend *see* Origin and History of Irish Names of Places, p 163.

Lorum, in Carlow: *Leamh-dhruim* (Lavrum), elm ridge.

Lough, a lake; an inlet of the sea.

Loughan (also Loughane, Loughaun), little lake.

Loughanreagh, grey little lake.

Loughbeg, little lake.

Lough Boderg, the lake of the red cow.

Lough Bofin, the lake of the white cow.

Loughbrickland, corrupted by changing *r* to *l*, and adding *d* (*see* p 7.) from *Loch-Bricrenn*, F. M., the lake of *Bricriu*, a chief of the first century.

Lough Conn, in Mayo: *Loch-Con*, F. M., the lake of the hound.

Lough Corrib, the correct Irish name is *Loch Orbsen*, F. M., which was corrupted by the attraction of the *c* sound in *Loch* to *Orbsen*, and by the omission of the syllable *sen*. *Orbsen* was another name for *Manannan Mac Lir*, a celebrated legendary personage.

Loughcrew, in Meath: *Loch-craeibhe* (creeve), the lake of the branchy tree.

Lough Derg, on the Shannon: contracted from *Loch-*

Dergdherc (Dergerk), the lake of the red eye, which is explained by a legend.

Lough Derravara, in Westmeath: *Loch-Dairbhreach* (Darravara), F. M., the lake of the oaks. *See* Darraragh.

Lough Erne, the lake of the *Ernai,* a tribe of people.

Lough Finn, *see* Finn river.

Lough Guitane, near Killarney: *Loch-coiteáin* (cut-thaun), the lake of the little *cot* or boat.

Lough Melvin, corrupted from *Loch-Meilghe* (Melye), the lake of *Meilghe,* an ancient king of Ireland.

Lough Neagh, written in the Book of Leinster *Loch-nEchach* (nehagh), the lake of *Eochy* (Ohy), a Munster chief, who was drowned in it at the time of its eruption in the first century. The *N* is a mere grammatical inflection, and the name is often used without it; for instance, we find it spelled *Lough Eaugh* in Camden, as well as in many of the maps of the 16th and 17th centuries.

Lough Oughter, in Cavan: *Loch-uachtar,* upper lake, i. e. upper as regards Lough Erne.

Loughrea, in Galway: *Loch-riabhach,* grey lake.

Lug, a hollow: *see* Lag.

Lugduff mountain, over Glendalough: black hollow, from a hollow at the base.

Luggelaw, the hollow of the *lagh* or hill.

Lugmore, great hollow.

Lugnaquillia, the highest mountain in Wicklow: *Lug-na-gcoilleach* (Lugnagulliagh), the hollow of the cocks, i. e. grouse.

Lumcloon, bare meadow (*lom,* bare).

Lurgan, the shin; a long hill.

Lurganboy, yellow long hill.

Lurraga, *see* Lurgan.

Lusk, in Dublin: *Lusca,* a cave.

Lusmagh, in King's County: the plain of herbs (*lus,* a herb).

Lynally. In the sixth century there was a forest here called the wood of Ela, and the church founded by St. Colman, about the year 590, was thence called *Lann-Ealla* (O'C. Cal.), the church of *Ela,* which has been anglicised to the present name.

Lynn, a form of *Lann,* a house or church.

Lyre, *Ladhar* (Lyre), a fork formed by rivers or glens. *See* Lear.

Mace, *Más* (Mauce), the thigh, a long low hill.

Mackan (also Mackanagh, Macknagh, Mackney), a place producing parsnips (*meacan,* a parsnip).

Macosquin, in Derry: corrupted from *Magh-Cosgrain* (Macosgran), F. M., *Cosgran's* plain.

Maghera, *Machaire,* a plain. Maghera in Down and Maghera in Derry are both contracted from *Machaire-ratha* (Maghera-raha), the plain of the fort.

Magherabeg, little plain.

Magheraboy, yellow plain.

Magheracloone, the plain of the *cloon* or meadow.

Magheraculmoney, the plain of the back (*cul*) of the shrubbery.

Magheradrool, in Down: *Machaire-eadarghabhal* (Maghera-addrool), the plain between the (river) forks (*eadar,* between, and *gabhal*). *See* Addergoole.

Magherahamlet, in Down: the plain of the *Tamlaght* or plague monument. *See* Tallaght.

Magheramenagh, middle plain (*meadhonach*).

Magheramore, great plain.

Magherareagh, grey plain (*riabhach*).

Maghery, a form of Maghera, a plain.

Magunihy, barony of, in Kerry: *Magh-gCoincinm* (Magunkinny), F. M., the plain of the O'Conkins.

Mahee island, in Strangford Lough: the island of St. *Mochaei* (Mohee), bishop, a disciple of St. Patrick, and the founder of Nendrum.

Maigue, a river in Limerick: called *Maigh* in the annals, i. e., the river of the plain.

Mallow, in Cork: called in the Annals *Magh-Ealla* (Moyalla), the plain of the river Allo, which was anciently the name of that part of the Blackwater flowing by the town. *See* Duhallow.

Manulla, in Mayo: *Magh-Fhionnalbha* (Mah-Innalva), Hy. F., Finalva's plain.

Massareene, in Antrim: *Más-a'-rioghna* (Massareena), the queen's hill.

Maul, *Meall,* a lump, a hillock.

Maum, *Madhm* (Maum), a high mountain pass.

Maumturk, the pass of the boars (*torc*).

Maw, *Magh,* a plain.

Maynooth, *Magh-Nuadhat* (Ma-nooat), F. M., *Nuadhat's* plain, from *Nuadhat,* king of Leinster, foster-father to Owen More king of Munster. *See* Bear.

Mayo, *Magh-eó* (Ma-ó), the plain of the yews. Full name *Magheó-na-Saxan,* F. M., Mayo of the Saxons, from a number of English monks settled there in the seventh century, by St. Colman, an Irish monk, after he had retired from the see of Lindisfarne.

Meelick, *Miliuc* (Meeluck), F. M., low marshy ground.

Meen, a mountain meadow.

Meenadreen, the mountain meadow of blackthorns.

Meenkeeragh, mountain meadow of the sheep.

Milleen, a little hillock. *See* Maul.

Moan, *Moin* (mone), a bog.

Moanduff, black bog.

Moanmore, great bog.

Moanroe, red bog.

Moanvane (also Moanvaun), *Moin-bhán,* white bog.

Moat, *Móta,* a high mound.

Moate, in Westmeath: from the great mound at the village; full name Moategranoge, the moat of *Graine-óg* or young Grace, who, according to tradition, was a Munster princess.

Mocollop, the plain *(magh)* of the *collops* or cattle.

Modeshill, *Magh-deisiol* (Ma-deshil), southern plain.

Mogeely, *Magh-Ile,* F. M., the plain of *Ile* or Ely.

Moher, *see* Cliffs of Moher.

Mohill, *Maethail* (Mwayhill), soft or spongy land; from *maeth,* soft.

Moig (also Moigh), forms of *Magh,* a plain.

Moira, *Magh-rath,* F. M., the plain of the forts.

Mon, *see* Moan.

Monabraher (also Monambraher, Monamraher), *Moin-na-mbrathar,* F. M., the bog of the friars.

Monagay, in Limerick: the bog of the goose *(gedh);* from wild geese.

Monaghan, *Muineachois,* F. M., a place full of little hills or brakes *(muine).*

Monamintra, in Waterford: *Moin-na-mbaintreabhaigh* (Monamointree), the bog of the widows.

Monard, high bog.

Monasteranenagh, in Limerick: *Mainister-an-aenaigh* (Monasteraneany), F. M., the monastery of the fair. Anciently called *Aenach-beag,* little fair.

Monasterboice, in Louth: the monastery of St. *Boethius* or *Buite,* who founded it in the sixth century.

Monasterevin, the monastery of St. Evin, the founder a contemporary of St. Patrick.

Monasteroris, in King's County: *Mainister-Fheorais, (orish: F* aspirated and omitted: *see* p 5.), the monastery of Mac *Feorais* or Bermingham, who founded it in A D 1325.

Monear, a meadow.

Moneen, a little bog *(moin).*

Money, *Muine* (munny), a shrubbery.

Moneydorragh, *Muine-dorcha,* dark or gloomy shrubbery.

Moneyduff, *Muine-dubh,* black shrubbery.

Moneygall, the shrubbery of the *Galls* or foreigners.

Moneygorm, *Muine-gorm,* blue shrubbery.

Moneymore, great shrubbery.

Monivea, in Galway: *Muine-an-mheadha* (Money-an-va), F. M., the shrubbery of the mead, a kind of drink.

Monroe, *Moin-ruadh,* red bog.

Montiagh (also Montiaghs), *Mointeach,* a boggy place.

Morgallion. A branch of the *Gailenga* (*see* Gallen), settled in Leinster, and a portion of them gave name to the territory of *Mor-Gailenga* or the great *Gailenga*, now the barony of Morgallion in Meath.

Mothel (also Mothell), *see* Mohill.

Mountmellick. The old anglicised name is *Montiagh-meelick*, the bogs or boggy land of the *meelick* or marsh. *See* Montiagh and Meelick.

Mourne mountains, in Down. The ancient name was *Beanna Boirche* (Banna-Borka), F. M., the peaks of the shepherd *Boirche*, who herded on these mountains the cattle of *Ross*, king of Ulster in the third century. About the middle of the twelfth century, a tribe of the Mac Mahons from Cremorne (*see* Cremorne), settled in the south of the present county of Down, and gave their tribe name of *Mughdhorna* (Mourna), to the barony of Mourne, and to the Mourne mountains.

Movilla, in Down: *Magh-bhile* (Ma-villa), O'C. Cal., the plain of the ancient tree.

Moville, in Donegal: *see* Movilla.

Moy, *Magh* (mah), a plain.

Moyacomb, in Wicklow: *Magh-da-chon* (Moy-a-con), F. M., the plain of the two hounds.

Moyaliff, in Tipperary: *Magh-Ailbhe* (Moyalva), F. M., *Ailbhe's* or Alva's plain.

Moyard, high plain.

Moyarget, *Magh-airgid*, the plain of silver.

Moyarta, in Clare: *Magh-fherta* (*fh* silent: see p 5), the plain of the grave.

Moycullen, in Galway: the plain of holly.

Moydow, in Longford: *Magh-dumha* (Moy-dooa), F. M., the plain of the burial mound.

Moygawnagh, in Mayo: written in the Book of Lecan, *Magh-gamhnach*, the plain of the milch cows.

Moyglass, green plain.

Moygoish. The descendants of *Colla Uais* (*see* Cremorne), were called *Ui mic Uais* (Ee-mic-Oosh), a portion of whom were settled in Westmeath, and gave their name to the barony of Moygoish.

Moyle, *Mael*, a bald or bare hill.

Moylough, the plain of the lake.

Moymore, great plain.

Moynalty, in Meath: *Magh-nealta* (Moynalta), the plain of the flocks (*ealta*).

Moyne, *Maighin* (Moin), a little plain.

Moynoe, in Clare: same as Mayo; the *n* is a grammatical accident.

Moynure, the plain of the yew (*iubhar*).

Moyrus, the plain of the *ros* or peninsula.

Moys, i. e. plains; from *magh*.

Muckamore, in Antrim: *Magh-comair* (Ma-cummer), F. M., the plain of the *cummer* or confluence (of the Six mile Water with Lough Neagh).

Muckanagh (also Muckenagh), *Muiceannach*, a resort of pigs; a place where pigs used to feed or sleep (from *muc*).

Muckelty (also Mucker, Muckera, Muckery), *see* Muckanagh.

Mucklagh, *Muclach*, *see* Muckanagh.

Muckinish, pig island.

Muckloon (Mucklone, Mucklin), *Muc-chluain*, pig meadow.

Muckno, in Monaghan: *Mucshnamh* (Mucknauv), F. M., the swimming place (*snamh*) of the pigs; the place where pigs used to swim across the little lake.

Muckross, the peninsula of the pigs.

Muff, a corruption of *Magh*, a plain.

Muing, a sedgy place.

Mullacrew, in Louth: *Mullach-craeibhe* (Mullacreeva), the summit of the spreading tree.

Mullagh, *Mullach*, a summit.

Mullaghareirk mountains, near Abbeyfeale in Limerick: *Mullach-a'-radhairc* (rīrk), the summit of the prospect.

Mullaghbane, white summit.

Mullaghboy, yellow summit.

Mullaghbrack, speckled summit.

Mullaghdoo (also Mullaghduff), black summit.

Mullaghglass, green summit.

Mullaghmeen, *Mullach-mín*, smooth summit.

Mullaghmore, great summit.

Mullaghroe, *Mullach-ruadh*, red summit.

Mullan (also Mullaun), a little *mullach* or summit.

Mullans, little summits.

Mullen (also Mullin), *Muileann* (mullen), a mill.

Mullinahone, in Tipperary: *Muileann-na-huamhainn* (Mullinahooan), the mill of the cave (*uamha*); from a cave near the village through which the little river runs.

Mullinavat, in Kilkenny: *Muilenn-a'-bhata*, the mill of the stick.

Mully, *see* Mullagh.

Multyfarnham, in Westmeath: *Muilte-Farannain* (Multy-Farannan), Farannan's mills (*muilenn*, plural *muille*).

Munster. Old Irish name *Mumhan* (Mooan), which, with *ster* added (*see* Leinster), forms *Mughan-ster* (Moon-ster) or Munster.

Murragh (also Murreagh), *Murbhach* (Murvagh), a flat marshy piece of land by the sea.

Murrow of Wicklow: *see* Murragh.

Muskerry. The people descended from Carbery Musc, son of Conary II. (*see* Corkaguiny), were called *Mus-*

craidhe (Muskery: O'Dugan). Of these there were several tribes, one of which gave name to the two baronies of Muskerry in Cork.

Myshall, in Carlow: *Muigh-íseal* (Mweeshal), low plain.

Naas, in Kildare, the most ancient residence of the kings of Leinster, *Nás* (Nawee), a fair or meeting place.

Nantinan, in Limerick: *Neantanán*, a place of nettles (*neanta*).

Nappan, in Antrim: *Cnapán*, a little hill.

Naul, in the north of Dublin, *'n-aill* (naul), the cliff. The article incorporated: *see* Nenagh.

Ned, *Nead* (Nad), a bird's nest.

Nenagh, in Tipperary. Irish name *Aenach* (Enagh), a fair; the *N* is a contraction for the Irish definite article 'an', which has become incorporated with the word: *'n-Aenach* (Nenagh), the fair. The full name is *Aenach-Urmhumlan* (Enagh-urooan) the fair of Ormond or east Munster, and this name is still used by those speaking Irish.

Newrath, *'n-Iubhrach* (Nuragh), the yew land; by the incorporation of the article.

New Ross. Irish name *Ros-mic-Treoin* (Rosmictrone), the wood (*ros*) of the son of *Treun*.

Newry. Ancient name *Iubhar-cinn-tragha* (Yure-Kin-traw), the yew tree at the head of the strand. In after ages this was shortened to *Iubhar*, which, with the article prefixed (*see* Nenagh), and *y* added, became changed to the present form Newry.

Nicker, in Limerick: *Cuinicér* (Knickere), a rabbit warren (from *coinín*).

Nobber, *Obair* (obber), work, with the article incorporated (*see* Nenagh): Nobber, 'the work', a name applied, according to tradition, to the English castle erected there.

Nohoyal, in Cork and Kerry: shortened from *Nuachong-bhail* (Nuhongval), new *congbhail* or habitation. *See* Conwal.

Nure, *see* Newry.

Nurney, in Kildare and Carlow: *Urnaidhe* (urny), F. M., a prayer house or oratory, with the article incorporated. *See* Nenagh and Urney.

Offaly, baronies of, in Kildare. The descendants of *Ros-failghe* (faly) or *Ros* of the rings, the eldest son of Cahirmore (king of Ireland from A D 120 to 123) were called *Hy Failghe* (O'Dugan), i. e. the descendants of *Failghe* (*see* Iverk), and a portion of their ancient inheritance still retains this name, in the modernized form Offaly.

Offerlane, in Queen's County: a tribe name; *Ui Foircheall-láin* (Hy Forhellane), F. M., the descendants (*ui*) of *Foircheallán.*

Oghill, *Eóchaill* (Oghill), yew wood (*eó* and *coill*).

Oneilland. *Niallán,* the fourth in descent from *Colla Da Chrioch* (cree) brother of Colla Meann (*see* Cremorne), was the progenitor of the tribe called *Hy Niallain* (i. e. Niallan's race), F. M., and their ancient patrimony forms the two baronies of Oneilland in Armagh, which retain the name. D added; *see* p 7.

Oola, in Limerick and Waterford: *Ubhla* (Oola), a place of apples, an orchard (from *ubhall* or *abhall*).

Oran, *Uaran* (uran) a cold spring.

Oranmore, in Galway: great cold spring.

Oughterard, upper height (*uachdar,* upper).

Oulart, in Wexford: *abhall-ghort* (oulort), an orchard, compounded of *abhall* and *gort.*

Ounageeragh river, flowing into the Funcheon: *Abh-na-gcaerach,* the river of the sheep.

Ovens, The, near Ballincollig in Cork: called in Irish *Uamhanna* (Oovana) i. e. the caves, from the great limestone caves near the village. The people by a slight change of pronunciation have converted these *oovans* or caves into *ovens. See* Athnowen.

Owbeg river, *Abh-beag,* little river.

Owenass river, at Mountmellick: the river of the cataract (*eas*).

Owenboy, yellow river (*abhainn*).

Owenclogy, stony river (*abhainn* and *cloch*).

Owenduff, black river.

Owenmore, *Abhainn-mór,* great river.

Owenreagh, grey river (*riabhach*).

Oxmanstown (also Ostmantown), in Dublin: so called because the Danes or Ostmen had a fortified settlement there.

Ox mountains: called in Irish *Sliabh-ghamh* (Slievegauv), F. M., the mountain of the storms, which in the spoken language was mistaken for *Sliabh-dhamh,* the mountain of the oxen, and translated accordingly.

Park, Irish *Pairc,* a field.

Parkmore, great field.

Phoenix Park, in Dublin, took its name from a beautiful spring well near the Viceregal Lodge, called *Fionn-uisg'* (feenisk), clear or limpid water.

Poll, a hole, pit, or pool.

Pollacappul, *Poll-a'-chapaill,* the hole of the horse.

Pollagh, a place full of holes or pits.

Pollanass, at Glendalough: the pool of the waterfall.

Pollans, holes, pools, or pits.

Pollaphuca, the *pooka's* or demon's hole.

Pollrone, in Kilkenny: *Poll-Ruadhain* (Ruan), *Ruadh-an's* hole.

Pollsallagh (also Pollsillagh), the hole of the sallows.

Portlaw, in Waterford: *Port-lagha,* the bank or landing place of the hill.

Portmarnock, St. Mernoc's bank or landing place.

Portnashangan, the *port,* bank, or landing place of the *seangans* or pismires.

Portraine, *see* Lambay island.

Portrush, in Antrim: *Port-ruis,* the landing place of the peninsula.

Portumna, in Galway: *Port-omna,* F. M., the landing place of the oak.

Pottle, in Cavan: a measure of land.

Preban (also Prebaun, Pribbaun), *Preabán,* a patch.

Pubble, *Pobul,* people, a congregation.

Pubblebrien, in Limerick: O'Brien's people; for it was the patrimony of the O'Briens.

Pullagh, a place full of holes.

Pullans (also Pullens), little holes or pits.

Quilcagh mountain at the source of the Shannon in Cavan, *Cailceach,* chalky; from its white face.

Quilly, *Coillidh* (cuilly), woodland.

Racavan, *Rath-cabhain,* the fort of the hollow.

Rahan, in King's County: *Raithin,* a ferny place.

Rahaniska (also Rahanisky), the rath of the water.

Rahard, *Rath-ard,* high fort.

Raharney, in Westmeath: *Rath-Athairne,* Aharny's fort.

Raheen, little rath or fort.

Raheenduff, black little fort.

Raheenroe, *Raithín-ruadh,* red little fort.

Rahelty, *Rath-eilte,* the fort of the doe (*eilit*).

Raheny, near Dublin: *Rath-Enna,* F. M., Enna's fort. 、

Rahugh, in Westmeath: the fort of St. *Aedh* or Hugh, the son of *Brec,* who built a church in the old rath in the sixth century.

Raigh, *see* Rath.

Rakeeragh, the fort of the sheep (*caera*).

Ramoan, in Antrim: *Rath-Modhain,* Modan's fort.

Ranaghan (also Rannagh), a ferny place (*raithne,* a fern).

Raphoe, in Donegal: *Rath-bhoth* (Ra-voh), F. M., the fort of the *boths,* tents, or huts.

Rasharkin, in Antrim: *Ros-Earcáin,* Erkan's promontory.

Rashee, in Antrim: *Rath-sithe* (Ra-shee) F. M., the fort of the fairies.

Ratass, in Kerry: *Rath-teas,* southern fort.

Rath, a circular fort.

Rathangan, in Kildare: *Rath-Iomghain* (Rath-Imgan), Imgan's fort.

Rathanny, *Rath-eanaighe*, the fort of the marsh.

Rathaspick, the fort of the bishop (*easpug*).

Rathbane (also Rathbaun), white rath.

Rathbeg, little fort.

Rathborney, in Clare: *Rath-boirne*, the fort of Burren, from its situation in the old district of Burren.

Rathcormack, Cormac's fort.

Rathdowney, in Queen's County: *Rath-tamhnaigh* (Rath-towney), F. M., the fort of the green field (*tamhnach*).

Rathdrum, the fort of the long hill.

Rathduff, black fort.

Rathfeigh, in Meath: the fort of the exercise green. *See* Faha.

Rathfryland, in Down: *see* p 7.

Rathglass, green fort.

Rathkeale, *Rath-Gaela*, Gaela's fort.

Rathkenny, *Rath-Cheannaigh* (Kanny), *Ceannach's* fort.

Rathkieran, in Kilkenny: Kieran's fort; from St. Kieran of Ossory. *See* Seirkieran.

Rathmore, great fort.

Rathmoyle, bald or dilapidated fort.

Rathmullan, *Rath-Maelain*, F. M., Maclan's rath.

Rathnew, in Wicklow, *Rath-Naoi*, F. M., *Naoi's* fort.

Rathreagh, *Rath-riabhach*, grey fort.

Rathroe, red fort.

Rathronan, Ronan's fort.

Rathsallagh, *Rath-salach*, dirty fort.

Rathvilly, in Carlow, *Rath-bile*, F. M., the fort of the old tree.

Rattoo, *Rath-tuaidh* (too), northern fort.

Raw, *Rath*, a fort.

Rea, *Reidh*, a coarse mountain flat.

Reask (also Reisk), *Riasg* (Reesk), a marsh.

Reen, *Rinn*, a point of land.

Relagh, *Reidhleach* (Relagh), *see* Rea.

Relickmurry, *Reilig*, a church: the church of the Blessed Virgin Mary.

Riesk, *see* Reask.

Rin (also Rine, Rinn), *Rinn*, a point of land.

Ring, *see* Rin.

Ringabella, near the mouth of Cork harbour: the point of the old tree (*bile*).

Ringagonagh, near Dungarvan: *Rinn-O' gCuana* (Ogoona), the point or peninsula of the O'Cooneys.

Ringbane (also Ringbaun), white point.

Ringcurran, near Kinsale: the point of the *corrán* or reaping hook; from its shape.

Ringrone, near Kinsale: written in the Annals of Innisfallen, *Rinn-róin*, the point of the seal.

Ringvilla (also Ringville), *Rinn-bhile* (villa), the point of the *bile* or ancient tree.

Rinneen, little point of land.

Rinville, in Galway: *Rinn-Mhil* (vil), the point of *Mil*, a Firbolg chieftain.

Risk, *see* Reask.

Roeillaun, *Ruadh-oilean* (Roo-illaun), red island.

Rooaun (also Rooghan, Rooghaun), reddish land (from *ruadh*, red).

Roosk, *Rusg*, a marsh. *See* Reask.

Roosca (also Rooskagh, Roosky), *Rusgach*, marshy, a marshy place.

Roscommon, *Ros-Comain*, F. M., Coman's wood, from St. *Coman*, who founded a monastery there in the eighth century.

Roscrea, written in the Book of Leinster, *Ros-cre*, *Cre's* wood.

Roshin, little *ros* or promontory.

Roskeen, *Ros-caein*, beautiful wood.

Ross, in the south generally means a wood; in the north, a peninsula.

Rossbegh (also Rossbehy), west of Killarney: the peninsula of birches (*beith*).

Rossbeg, small wood or promontory.

Ross Carbery, in Cork: the latter part from the barony of Carbery in which it is situated: it was anciently called *Ros-ailithir* (allihir), F. M., the wood of the pilgrims.

Ross Castle, at Killarney: from the little *ros* or peninsula on which it stands.

Rosses, in Donegal: i. e. peninsulas.

Rossinver, in Leitrim: *Ros-inbhir*, the peninsula of the river mouth; from a point of land running into the south part of Lough Melvin.

Rossmore, great wood or peninsula.

Rossorry, near Enniskillen: corrupted from *Ros-airthir* (arher) F. M., the eastern peninsula.

Roughan (also Ruan), *see* Rooaun.

Rousky, *see* Roosca and Rooskey.

Route. The northern part of Antrim was anciently called *Dalriada* (F. M.), i. e. *Riada's* portion or tribe, from Carbery Riada, son of Conary II. (*see* Corkaguiny), and the latter part (*Riada*) of this old name, is still preserved in the corrupted form of Route.

Rush, in Dublin: *Ros-eo* (Rush-oï), F. M., the peninsula of the yew trees.

Rusheen, small wood; a growth of underwood.

Russagh, *Ros-each*, F. M., the wood of the horses.

Rusky, *see* Roosca and Roosky.

Saggart, in Dublin: contracted from Tassagard, Irish *Teach-Sacra* (Tassacra), O'C. Cal., the house of St. *Sacra*, who flourished in the seventh century.

Saint Mullins, in Carlow: Irish name *Tigh-Moling* (Tee-Molling), O'C. Cal., the house of St. *Moling*, a native of Kerry, who erected a church there about the middle of the seventh century. *See* Timolin.

Salt, baronies of, in Kildare: *see* Leixlip.

Santry, in Dublin: *Sentreibh* (Shantrev; Mart. Taml.), old tribe.

Saul, near Downpatrick: *Sabhall* (Saul), a barn. *Dichu*, the prince of the surrounding district, was St. Patrick's first convert in Ireland. The chief made the saint a present of his barn, to be used temporarily as a church, and hence the place was called *Sabhall-Patrick*, St. Patrick's barn, now shortened to Saul.

Scalp, *Scealp* (Scalp), a cleft or chasm.

Scarawalsh, in Wexford: Irish name *Sgairbh-a'-Breathnaigh* (Scarriff-a-vranny), Walsh's scarriff or shallow ford (see Ballybrannagh), which, with an obvious alteration, has given name to the barony of Scarawalsh.

Scardan (also Scardaun), *Scardan*, a cataract.

Scarriff, *Scairbh* (Scarriv), a rugged shallow ford.

Scart, *Scairt* (Scart), a thicket or cluster.

Scartaglin, in Kerry: the thicket of the glen.

Scarteen, a little thicket or cluster.

Scartlea, in Cork: *Scairt-liath*, grey thicket.

Scarva, another form of Scarriff.

Seagoe, *Suidhe-Gobha* (Seegow), the seat of St. *Gobha* (gow) or Gobanus.

Seapatrick, Patrick's seat (*suidhe*)

See, *suidhe* (see), a seat or sitting place.

Seefin, *Suidhe-Finn* (Seefin), the seat of Finn Mac Coole.

Seein, in Tyrone: same as Seefin, with *f* aspirated and omitted (*Suidhe-Fhinn*).

Seirkieran, near Parsonstown. St. *Ciaran* or Kieran of Ossory, disciple of St. Finnian of Clonard, erected a monastery in the sixth century, at a place called *Saighir* (Sair), which was the name of a fountain, and after the saint's time it was called *Saighir-Chiarain* (Sairkeeran), now contracted to Seirkieran.

Seltan, a place of sallows.

Seskin, *Sescenn*, a marsh.

Sessia (also Sessiagh), *Seiseadh* (shesha), the sixth part.

Shallon, *Sealán*, a hangman's rope, a gallows.

Shan, *Sean* (shan), old.

Shanaclogh, *Seancloch*, old stone castle.

Shanacloon, old cloon or meadow.

Shanagarry, old *garry* (*garrdha*) or garden.

Shanagolden, in Limerick: *Seangualann* (Shanagoolan), old shoulder or hill.

Shanakill, old church.

Shanavally (also Shanbally), old *bally* or town.

Shanbogh (also Shanbo), old *both* or tent.

Shandon, old *dun* or fortress.

Shandrum, old *drum* or ridge.

Shangarry, *see* Shanagarry.

Shankill, old church.

Shanmullagh, old *mullach* or summit.

Shantallow, *Sean-talamh* (Shantalav), old land.

Shanvally, old *bally* or town (*b* aspirated).

Shean (also Sheean, Sheeaun), *Sidheán* (sheeaun), a fairy hill.

Shee, *sidh* (shee), a fairy, a fairy hill.

Sheeroe, red fairy hill.

Sheetrim, *Sidh-dhruim* (Sheedrim), fairy ridge.

Shelburne barony, in Wexford: from the tribe of *Siol-Brain* (O'Dugan), the seed of progeny of *Bran*.

Shelmaliere, in Wexford: the descendants of Maliere or *Maelughra* (Meelura).

Sheskin, *Sescenn*, a marsh. See Seskin.

Shillelagh, in Wicklow: *Siol-Elaigh* (Sheelealy: O'Dugan), the seed or descendants of *Elach*.

Shinrone, in King's County: *Suidhe-an-róin* (Sheenrone), F. M., the seat of the *ron*, i. e. literally a seal, but figuratively a hirsute or hairy man.

Shrone, *srón*, a nose, a pointed hill.

Shruel (also Shrule), *see* p 7.

Sion, *sidheán* (sheeaun), a fairy mount.

Skagh, *Sceach*, a white thorn bush.

Skahanagh (also Skehanagh), a place full of *sceachs* or white thorns.

Skeagh (also Skea), *see* Skagh.

Skeheen, a little *sceach* or bush.

Skelgagh, a place of *skelligs* or rocks.

Skellig rocks, off the coast of Kerry: *Sceilig* means a rock.

Skerries (also Skerry), *Sceir* (sker), a sea rock; *sceire* (skerry), sea rocks.

Skreen (also Skrine), *Scrín* (skreen), a shrine.

Sleaty, in Queen's County: *sleibhte* (Sleaty), F. M., i. e. mountains, the plural of *sliabh*: from the adjacent hills of *Slieve* Margy.

Slee, *Slighe* (slee), a road.

Slemish mountain, in Antrim, on which St. Patrick passed his youth herding swine, *Sliabh-Mis*, the mountain of *Mis*, a woman's name.

Sleveen, little *slieve* or mountain.

Slieve, *Sliabh* (sleeve), a mountain.

Slieve Anierin, in Leitrim: *Sliabh-an-iarainn*, the mountain of the iron; from its richness in iron ore.

Slievebane (also Slievebaun), white mountain.

Slievebeagh, a range of mountains on the borders of Monaghan, Fermanagh, and Tyrone: *Sliabh-Beatha* (Slieve Baha), F. M., the mountain of *Bith,* a legendary hero.

Slieve Bernagh, in the east of Clare: *Sliabh-bearnach,* gapped mountain. *See* Lisdoonvarna.

Slievebloom, *Sliabh-Bladhma* (Slieve-Blawma), F. M., the mountain of *Bladh* (Blaw), one of the Milesian heroes.

Slieveboy, yellow mountain.

Slieve Corragh, rugged mountain.

Slieve Donard, the highest of the Mourne mountains. *Domhanghart* (Donart), son of the king of Ulidia, and one of St. Patrick's disciples, built a little church on the very summit of this mountain; hence it was called *Sliabh-Domhanghart, Donart's* mountain, now anglicised Slieve Donard. Its ancient name was Slieve Slanga, from the bardic hero *Slainge,* the son of Parthalon, who was buried on its summit, where his carn is still to be seen.

Slieve Eelim, a mountain range east of Limerick: *Sliabh-Eibhlinne* (Slieve-Evlinne), Evlin's mountain.

Slieve Fuad, near Newtownhamilton in Armagh: Fuad's mountain; from the Milesian hero Fuad, who was slain there.

Slieve League, in Donegal: *Sliabh-liag,* the mountain of the flag-stones.

Slieve Lougher, east of Castleisland in Kerry: *Sliabh-luachra,* rushy mountain.

Slieve Mish, near Tralee: *see* Slemish.

Slievenagriddle, near Downpatrick: the mountain of the griddle; the *griddle* is a *cromlech* on the hill.

Slievenamon, in Tipperary: *Sliabh-na-mban,* the mountain of the women. Full name *Sliabh-na-mban-Feimhinn* (Slievenamon-Fevin), the mountain of the women of *Feimheann,* the ancient territory surrounding it.

Slievenamuck, the mountain of the pigs.

Slievereagh, *Sliabh-riabhach,* grey mountain.

Slieveroe, red mountain.

Slievesnaght, the mountain of the snow (*sneacht*).

Sligo, named from the river: *Sligeach* (Sliggagh), F. M., shelly river (*slig,* a shell).

Sliguff, a corruption (*see* p 7.) from *Slighe-dhubh* (Slee-duv), a black road.

Slyne Head, in Galway: Irish name *Ceann-leama* (Can-leama), the head of the *lyme* or leap (*leim*), which has been corrupted to the present name by changing *m* to *n,* and prefixing *s. See* Stabannon.

Solloghod, in Tipperary: *Sulchoid* (sollohed), F. M., sallow wood.

Sonnagh, a mound or rampart.

Sragh (also Srah), *srath* (srah), a river holm.

Srahan (also Srahaun, Sraheen), little river holm.

Sroohill, *see* p 7.

Srough, *Sruth* (sruh), a stream.

Sroughmore, great *sruth* or stream.

Sruffaun, *Sruthán* (Sruhaun), a streamlet (p 7.).

Stabannon, corrupted from Tabannon, Bannon's house (*teach*), by prefixing *s. See* Slyne head.

Stakallen, in Meath: *Teach-Collain* (Tacollan), F. M., Collan's house.

Staholmog, in Meath: St. *Colmoc's* or *Mocholmoc's* house.

Stamullin, in Meath: *Maelan's* house.

Stang, a measure of land.

Stillorgan, in Dublin: *Tigh-Lorcain* (Teelorcan), *Lorcan's* or Laurence's house or church.

Stonecarthy, in Kilkenny: first syllable a corruption of *stang*: Carthy's *stang* or measure of land.

Stonybatter, in Dublin: stony road: *see* Batterstown and Booterstown.

Stook, *Stuaic* (stook), a pointed pinnacle.

Stookan (also Stookeen), a little *stook* or pointed rock.

Stradbally, *Stradbhaile* (Sradvally), F. M., street-town; a town of one street.

Stradone (also Stradowan), *Srath-doimhin* (Sradowan), deep *srath*' or river holm.

Stradreagh, grey street.

Straduff, black river holm.

Straffan, in Kildare: *see* Sruffaun.

Straid (also Strade, Sraud), *Sráid* (Sraud), a street.

Strancally, near Youghal: *Sron-caillighe* (Srone-cally), the hag's nose or point.

Strangford Lough, in Down: a Danish name; *strong fiord* or bay, from the well-known tidal currents at its entrance. Irish name *Loch Cuan.*

Struell, *see* p 7.

Sylaun, a place of sallows.

Taghadoe, in Kildare: *Teach-Tuae* (Taghtoo), F. M., the house of St. Tua.

Taghboy, yellow house.

Taghmon, in Wexford: written in the Book of Leinster *Teach-Munna* (Taghmunna), the house of St. Munna or Fintan, who founded a monastery there, and died in A D 634.

Tallaght, in Dublin: *Taimhleacht* (Tavlaght), a plague monument. According to the bardic legend, 9000 of Parthalon's people died of the plague, and were buried in this place, which was therefore called the *Taimhleacht* or plague grave of Parthalon's people.

Tamlaght (also Tamlat), a plague grave; *see* Tallaght.

Tamnagh (also Tamny), *Tamhnach*, a green field.

Tanderagee, a corruption of *Tóin-re-gaeith* (Tonregee), *backside* to the wind. See Tonlegee.

Tara, *Teamhair* (Tawer), F. M., a residence on an elevated spot, commanding an extensive view. There are many places of this name in Ireland, besides the celebrated Tara in Meath.

Tarmon, *see* Termon.

Tat (also Tate, Tath), a measure of land.

Tattygare, short *tate* or land measure.

Taughboyne, in Donegal: *Tech-Baeithin* (Taghbweeheen), O'C. Cal., the house of St. *Baeithin;* he was a companion of St. Columkille, and governed the monastery of Iona after that saint's death. Died in A D 600.

Tavanagh (also Tavnagh), *Tamhnach*, a green field.

Tawlaght, a plague monument. *See* Tallaght.

Tawnagh (also Tawny), *Tamhnach*, a green field.

Tawnaghmore, great field.

Tecolm, in Queen's County: *Tigh-Choluim* (Teecolum). St. Columkille's house.

Teebane, *Tigh-bán* (Teebaun), white house.

Teemore, great house (*tigh*).

Teev (also Teeve), *Taebh*, the side, a hill side.

Teltown, on the blackwater in Meath. Lewy of the long hand, one of the Tuatha De Danann kings, established a fair or gathering of the people, to be held here yearly on the first of August, in which games, pastimes, and marriages were celebrated; and in honour of his foster mother *Taillte* (Telta), he called the place *Tailltenn* (Teltenn), now modernized to Teltown.

Temple, *Teampull*, a church.

Templeachally, in Tipperary: the church of the *cala* or marshy meadow.

Templebredon, in Tipperary: O'Bredon's church.

Templebreedy, St. Brigid's church.

Templecarn, in Donegal: the church of the carn or monument.

Temple-etney, in Tipperary: St. Eithne's church.

Templemichael, the church of the Archangel Michael.

Templemolaga, in Cork: the church of St. *Molaga*, a native of Fermoy, who died on the 20th of January, some short time before the year 664.

Templemore, great church; a cathedral.

Templemoyle, bald or dilapidated church (*mael*).

Templenacarriga, the church of the rock.

Templenoe (also Templenew), *Teampull-nua*, new church.

Templepatrick, St. Patrick's church.

Templeport, the church of the *port* or bank.

Templeshanbo, in Wexford. Ancient pagan name *Sean-both-Sine* (Shanboh-Sheena), *Sin's* or Sheen's old tent or hut. In Christian times, after a church had been erected there, the present name was formed by the addition of the word *Temple* to *Seanboth:* Templeshanbo, the church of *Seanboth*.

Templetogher, in Galway: the church of the causeway (*tóchar*), from a celebrated old *togher* across a bog.

Templetuohy, in Tipperary: the church of the *tuath* or territory, because it was the principal church of the district.

Tempo, in Fermanagh: shortened from the full Irish name *an t-Iompodh-deisiol* (an Timpo deshill), the turning from left to right. *Iompodh* (impo) means turning, *deisiol*, right handed, and the article *an* prefixed takes a *t* in this case, which became incorporated with the word. The place received its name, no doubt, from the ancient custom of turning sun-ways in worship.

Terenure, *Tir-an-iubhair*, the land of the yew.

Termon, *Tearmann*, church land.

Termonfeckin, St. *Fechin's* church land.

Terryglass, in Tipperary: called in Irish authorities *Tir-da-ghlas* (Tir-a-glas), which Adamnan in his Life of St. Columba translates *Ager-duorum-rivorum*, the land of the two streams.

Thurles, in Tipperary: *Durlios* (Durlas), strong *lis* or fort. In the annals it is commonly called Durlas-O'Fogarty, from the O'Fogartys, the ancient proprietors of the surrounding district. *See* Eliogarty.

Tiaquin, barony of, in Galway: shortened from *Tigh-Dachonna* (Tee-aconna), F. M., St. Dachonna's house.

Tibberaghny, in Kilkenny: *Tiobrad-Fachtna* (Tibbradaghna), F. M., St. Faghna's well

Tibohine, in Roscommon: *Tech-Baeithin* (O'Cal. Cal.), St. *Baeithin's* house. The name is the same as Taughboyne, but this is a different *Baeithin*; he was of the race of *Enda*, son of Niall of the Nine Hostages, and was one of the ecclesiastics to whom the apostolic letter was written in the year 640, on the subject of the time for celebrating Easter.

Tieve, *Taebh* (teeve), a side, a hill-side.

Tievebrack, speckled hill-side.

Tiglin, in Wicklow: the house of the glen.

Tiknock (also Ticknock, Ticknick), *Tigh-cnuic* (Ticknick), the house of the hill.

Timahoe, in Queen's County: *Tech-Mochua* (Tee-Mohua), O'C. Cal., the house of St. *Mochua*, the original founder and patron, who flourished in the sixth century.

Timogue, in Queen's County: St. Mogue's house.

Timoleague, in Cork: *Teach-Molaga*, F. M., *Molaga's* house, from St. Molaga of Templemolaga.

Timolin, in Kildare: *Tigh-Moling* (Tee-Moling), St. Moling's house, from a church erected there by St. Moling of St. Mullins.

Tinamuck, *Tigh-na-muc*, the house of the pigs.

Tincurragh (also Tincurry), *Tigh-an-churraigh* (Tincurry), the house of the *currach* or marsh.

Tinnahinch (also Tinnehinch), *Tigh-na-hinnse* (Tee-na-hin-sha), the house of the island or river meadow.

Tinnakill (also Tinnakilly), the house of the church or wood.

Tinnascart (also Tinnascarty), the house of the cluster or thicket (*scairt*).

Tinnick (also Tinnock, Tinock), *see Tiknock*.

Tipper, a form of *Tobar*, a well.

Tipperary, *Tiobraid-Arann* (Tibrad-Auran), F. M., the well of *Ara*, the ancient territory in which it was situated. The well that gave this name to the town and thence to the county, was situated in the Main-street, but it is now closed up.

Tipperkevin, in Kildare: St. Kevin's well.

Tipperstown, in Dublin and Kildare: a half translation from *Baile-an-tobair* (Ballintubber), the town of the well.

Tiranascragh, in Galway: *Tir-an-eascrach*, the land of the *esker* or sand hill.

Tirawly, barony of, in Mayo: *Tir-Amha gaidh* (Awly), the land or district of *Amhalgaidh*, king of Connaught, brother of the monarch *Dathi*, and son of Ohy Moyvane, king of Ireland from A D 358 to 365.

Tirconnell, the ancient name of Donegal, *Tir-Conaill*, the land or district of Conall Gulban, son of Niall of the Nine Hostages.

Tireragh, barony of, in Sligo, *Tir-Fhiachrach* (Tir-eeragh), F. M., the district of *Fiachra*, son of *Dathi*, and grandson of Ohy Moyvane. *See* Tirawly.

Tirerrill, barony of, in Sligo, *Tir-Oiliolla* (ollila), Hy F., the district of Olioll, son of Ohy Moyvane (*see* Tirawly). *L* changed to *r: see* p 7.

Tirkeeran, barony of, in Derry: *Tir-Chaerthainn* (Tir-keerin), the district of Kieran, the great grandson of *Colla Uais*, brother of *Colla Meann*. *See* Cremorne.

Tisaran, in King's County: from an old church which is called in the Calendars *Teach-Sarain* (Tasaran), the house of St. Saran, the founder, who was of the race of the *Dealbhna*. *See* Delvin.

Tisaxon, the house of the Saxons or Englishmen.

Tiscoffin, in Kilkenny: *see* p 7.

Tober, *Tobar*, a well.

Toberaheena, the well of Friday (*aeine*, pron. eena); from the custom of visiting the well and performing devotions on Friday.

Toberbilly, the well of the ancient tree (*bile*).

Tobercurry, in Sligo: written by Mac Firbis, *Tober-an-choire*, the well of the caldron or pit.

Tobermore, great well.

Toberreendoney, in various counties: *Tobar-righ-an-domhnaigh* (Toberreendowny), the well of the king of Sunday (i. e. of God); these wells were so called because they were visited on Sunday.

Togher, *Tóchar*, a causeway.

Tomdeely, in Limerick: the tumulus (*tuaim*) of the river Deel.

Tomfinlough, in Clare: *Tuaim-Fionnlocha*, F. M., the tumulus of the bright lake (*fionn*, bright, clear); from an old church by a lake near Sixmile-bridge.

Tomgraney, in Clare: *Tuaim-greine* (Toomgraney), F. M., the tumulus of the lady *Grian*, about whom there are many traditions.

Tomies mountain, over the lower lake of Killarney, *Tumaidhe* (Toomy), tumuli or monumental mounds; from two sepulchral heaps on the top of the mountain.

Tomregan, in Cavan: *Tuaim-Drecon* (Toom-reckon: *D aspirated–see* p 5.), F. M., Drecon's burial mound.

Tonagh, *Tamhnach* (Townagh), a field.

Tonbane (also Tonbaun), white *tóin* or *backside*.

Tonduff, black *backside* (*tóin*).

Tonlegee, *Tóin-le-gaeith*, backside to the wind.

Tonnagh, a mound or rampart.

Tonregee, *see* Tanderagee and Tonlegee.

Tonroe, red backside.

Tooman, *Tuaman*, a small tumulus.

Toome (also Toom), *Tuaim* (Toom), a tumulus or burial mound.

Toomore (also Toomour), *Tuaim-dha-bhodhar* (Toom-a-wour), F. M., the tumulus of the two deaf persons.

Toomyvara, in Tipperary, exactly represents the sound of the Irish *Tuaim-ui-Mheadhra*, the tumulus or tomb of O'Mara.

Toor, *Tuar*, a bleach green or drying place.

Toorard, high bleach green.

Tooreen, little bleach green.

Toormore, great bleach green.

Toortane (also Toortaun), *Tortan*, a small hillock.

Tor, a tower, a tall tower-like rock.

Torc mountain at Killarney, the mountain of the *torcs* or boars.

Tormore, great tower or tower-like rock.

Tory island off the coast of Donegal, *Torach* (Wars of

GG.), towery, i. e. abounding in *tors* or tower-like rocks.

Touaghty, in Mayo: *Tuath-Aitheachta (Thoo-ahaghta), Hy. F., the tuath* or district of the *attacotti* or plebeians, i. e. the races vanquished and enslaved by the Milesians.

Tourin, little bleach green; *see* Tooreen.

Tralee, *Traigh-Li* (Tralee), F. M., the strand of the Lee, a little river which runs into the sea at the town, but which is now covered over.

Tramore, *Traigh-mor*, great strand.

Trean (also Trien), *Trian*, a third part.

Treanbaun, white third.

Treanboy, yellow third.

Treanlaur, middle third (*lár*, middle).

Treanmanagh, middle third (*meadhonach*).

Trevet, in Meath: *Trefoit* (Trefote), F. M., three *fods* or sods; so named, according to the *Leabhar-na-huidhre*, because when Art, the son of Conn of the Hundred Battles was buried there, three sods were dug over his grave in honour of the Trinity.

Trillick, *Tri-liag*, three *liags* or pillar stones.

Trim, in Meath full name *Ath-truim* (Ah-trim), the ford of the elder bushes.

Bridge and Castle, Trim

Tromaun, a place producing elder bushes (*trom*).

Trough, barony of, in Monaghan, *Triucha* (Truha), a cantred or district.

Trumman (also Trummery) *see* Tromaun.

Tuam, in Galway: *Tuaim-da-ghualann* (Tuam-a-woolan), the tumulus of the two shoulders, from the shape of the old sepulchral mound that gave name to the place.

Tubbrid, *see* Tober.

Tulla (also Tullach), *Tulach*, a little hill.

Tullaghan, a little *tulach* or hill.

Tullaghmelan, in Tipperary: Moylan's hill.

Tullahogue, in Tyrone: *Tulach-og*, F. M., the hill of the youths.

Tullahaught, in Kilkenny: *Tulach-ocht*, the hill of the eight (persons).

Tullamore, great hill.

Tullig, another form of *Tulach*, a hill.

Tullow, *Tulach*, a little hill.

Tullowphelim, a parish containing the town of Tullow in Carlow; contracted from Tullow-offelimy, the *tulach* or hill of the territory of the Hy Felimy, a tribe descended and named from Felimy, son of Enna Kinsella, king of Leinster in the fourth century.

Tully, *see* Tulla.

Tullyallen, *Tulaigh-áluinn* (Tullyaulin), beautiful hill.

Tullyard, high hill.

Tullybane (also Tullybaun), *Tulaigh-bán*, white hill.

Tullybeg, little *tulach* or hill.

Tullycorbet, the hill of the chariot (*carbad*).

Tullyglass, green hill.

Tullyhaw, barony of, in Cavan: so called from the Magaurans, its ancient proprietors, whose tribe name was *Tealach-Echach* (Tulla-eha: O'Dugan), the family of *Eochy* or Ohy.

Tullylease, in Cork: *Tulach-lias* (Tullaleese), the hill of the huts.

Tullymongan, at Cavan: *Tulach-Mongain*, F. M., Mongan's hill.

Tullymore, *see* Tullamore.

Tullynacross, the hill of the cross.

Tullynagardy, near Newtownards: *Tulaigh-na-gceard cha*, the hill of the forges.

Tullynaskeagh, the hill of the white thorns.

Tullynure, *Tulach-an-iubhair*, the hill of the yew.

Tullyroe, red hill.

Tullyrusk, in Antrim: the hill on which the old church stands was surrounded by marshy ground, hence the name, which Colgan writes *Tulach-ruisc*, the hill of the morass. *See* Rusk.

Tullytrasna, cross or transverse hill.

Tumna, in Roscommon: *Tuaim-mna*, F. M., the tomb of the woman (*bean*, gen. *mna*).

Tuosist, in Kerry: *Tuath-O'Siosta* (O'Sheesta), O'Siosta's territory.

Ture, the yew. The word *iubhar* (yure) has incorporated the *t* of the article, like Tempo.

Turlough, a lake that dries up in summer.

Twelve Pins, a remarkable group of mountains in Connemara; should have been called the Twelve *Bens*, i. e. peaks. Sometimes called 'The Twelve Pins of Bunnabola,' in which the word *beann* occurs twice; for Bunnabola is *Beanna-Beola* (Banna-Bola), the peaks of *Beola*, an old Firbolg chief, who is still remembered in tradition. *See* Mourne.

Tyfarnham, in Westmeath: *Farannan's* house (*tigh*); the same person that gave name to Multyfarnham.

Tyrone, in Tipperary: *Tigh-Eóin*, John's house.

Tyrella, in Down: *Tech-Riaghla* (Tee-Reela), O'C. Cal. the house of St. *Riaghal* (Reeal) or Regulus.

Tyrone. The descendants of *Eoghan* (Owen), son of Niall of the Nine Hostages, possessed the territory extending over the counties of Tyrone and Derry and the two baronies of Raphoe and Inishowen in Donegal; all this district was anciently called *Tir-Eoghain* (Tir-Owen: Wars of GG.), Owen's territory, which is now written Tyrone, and restricted to one county. *See* Inishowen.

Ulster, ancient Irish form *Uladh* (ulla), which with *ster* added (*see* Leinster), was pronounced *Ulla-ster*, and contracted to Ulster.

Ummera (also Ummery, Umry), *Iomaire* (Ummera), a ridge.

Ummeracam (also Umrycam), *Iomaire-cam*, crooked ridge.

Ummerafree, the ridge of the heath (*fraech*).

Unshinagh (also Inshinagh), *Uinseannach*, a place producing ash trees (*uinnse* and *fuinnse*).

Uragh, *Iubhrach* (yuragh), yew land.

Urbal, a tail; from shape or position.

Urbalreagh, in Antrim, Donegal, and Tyrone: grey tail.

Urbalshinny, in Donegal: the fox's tail (*sionnach*), from some peculiarity of shape, or perhaps from having been a resort of foxes.

Urcher, *Urchur*, a cast or throw. *See* Ardnurcher.

Uregare, in Limerick: *Iubhar-ghearr* (yure-yar), short yew tree.

Urney (also Urny), *Urnaidhe* (Urny), an oratory. *See* Nurney.

Urlar (also Urlaur), a floor, a level place.

Valentia Island, in Kerry: so called by the Spaniards. Ancient and present Irish name, *Dairbhre* (Darrery), a place producing oaks. *See* Kildorrery.

Vartry river, in Wicklow: a corruption of the old tribe name *Fir-tire* (Firteera), the men of the territory (*tir*).

Ventry, in Kerry: got its name from a beautiful white strand, called in Irish *Fionn-traigh* (Fintra), white strand.

Wateresk, upper channel (*eisc*). *See* Kilwatermoy.

Waterford, a Danish name; old form Vadrefiord, the latter part of which is the northern word *fiord*, a sea inlet. Old Irish name *Port-Lairge* or Portlargy *See* Strangford and Carlingford.

Watergrasshill, in Cork: a translation of the Irish name.

Cnocán-na-biolraighe (Knockaun-na-billery), the little hill of the water-cresses.

Wexford, a Danish name; old form Weisford, which is said to mean west *fiord* or bay; old Irish name, *Carman.*

Wicklow, a Danish name; old forms of the name, Wky-ynglo, Wygyngelo, Wykinlo. Old Irish name Kilmantan, the church of St. Mantan, one of St. Patrick's disciples. This saint, according to the Annals of Clonmacnoise and other authorities, had his front teeth knocked out by a blow of a stone, from one of the barbarians who opposed St. Patrick's landing in Wicklow; hence he was called *Mantan,* or the toothless.

Windgap (also Windygap), a translation of *Bearna-na-gaeithe* (Barnanageehy), the gap of the wind.

Witter, in Down: *Uachdar,* upper. *See* Wateresk and Eighter.

Wood of O, near Tullamore in King's County: the Irish name is *Eóchaill,* yew-wood, the same as Youghal: modern name an attempted translation: Wood of O, i. e. the wood of the *eó* or yew.

Yellow Batter, and **Green Batter,** near Drogheda: batter here means a road. *See* Booterstown and Batterstown.

Yewer, near Killashandra in Cavan: an anglicised form of *Iubhar* (yure), the yew tree. *See* Newry.

Youghal, in Cork. A yew wood grew anciently on the hill slope now occupied by the town, and even yet some of the old yews remain; hence it was called *Eochaill* (Oghill), F. M., i. e. yew wood. *See* Oghill and Aughall.